This is a fascinating book and a mu[...]
share the Greatest Story Ever Told.
Martin Goldsmith shares some rich
storytelling. Warning – this book contains gems.
Ian Coffey, speaker and author

Martin Goldsmith is a superb speaker. He writes like he speaks.
This is gripping stuff, showing the power of storytelling. Preachers
in this postmodern age should major on stories, but they don't.
Martin shows us how to do it – to patients in a doctor's waiting
room, to Muslims in a bus, or drunken youths in Thailand. His
extensive missionary experience, his Jewish background and his
deep understanding of other faiths have produced one of the most
fascinating and important books I have read for years. Buy two –
and give one away.
Michael Green, speaker and author

Goldsmith reminds us that 'The call to come to Jesus and follow
him must never be separated from his determination to make us
"fishers of men and women".' But how can we be more effective
as the Lord's fishermen? Martin's own batch of 'stories' shows
convincingly that the good news of Jesus is more likely to capture
people's minds and hearts through personal, emotionally gripping
stories. He reminds us that the example of the media and our
politicians should move us to try declaring our faith through
well-crafted, practised storytelling.

As Goldsmith learned in Malaysia and Indonesia, people tend to
remember stories even years after they've heard them. Stories are
the ideal form of communication in countries where the law forbids
forthright Christian witness or where hostility from those prejudiced
against the Christian faith prevents them from taking our witness
seriously. He convinced me!
Greg Livingstone, Founder, Frontiers

storytelling

ivp

storytelling

sharing the gospel with **passion** and **power**

Martin Goldsmith

INTER-VARSITY PRESS
Norton Street, Nottingham NG7 3HR, England
Email: ivp@ivpbooks.com
Website: www.ivpbooks.com

First published 2014

British Library Cataloguing in Publication Data
A catalogue record for this book is available from the British Library.

ISBN: 978–1–78359–155–8

Set in Dante 12/15pt
Typeset in Great Britain by CRB Associates, Potterhanworth, Lincolnshire
Printed and bound in Great Britain by Ashford Colour Press Ltd, Gosport,
Hampshire

*Inter-Varsity Press publishes Christian books that are true to the Bible and that
communicate the gospel, develop discipleship and strengthen the church for its mission
in the world.*

*Inter-Varsity Press is closely linked with the Universities and Colleges Christian
Fellowship, a student movement connecting Christian Unions in universities and colleges
throughout Great Britain, and a member movement of the International Fellowship of
Evangelical Students. Website: www.uccf.org.uk*

CONTENTS

A story can change a church

The beautiful West of England countryside stretched out on either side of the road. The sun was shining warmly, making the vivid yellow of the rape fields dazzle the eyes with their brightness. I was in very good time for the start of the church's international weekend at which I was to be the speaker. So there was no need to drive fast and I could allow my mind to picture what sort of church it would be.

A combination of the net and personal emails had given the impression of a nice little evangelical Anglican congregation in a big old traditional church building in the very centre of the city. In another part of town a large well-known moderately charismatic congregation stole all the limelight, so the city-centre church would feel its ineffectiveness all the more and would wonder what role it was called to play in God's overall purposes. The dominating size of the church building would make the little congregation of about seventy Christians feel all the more insignificant.

As I prayed about the forthcoming weekend, the question stood out: what part should this weekend have in stimulating the congregation not only in their wider mission concern for the work of God overseas, but also for their mission in their community locally?

Seminars on the Saturday set the tone for the weekend. The Holy Spirit remains alive and active in our times. He is working amazingly in many parts of the world and he surely longs also to reveal the glory of Jesus to the multitudes of our own country and city here. Neither the secular pluralistic world nor the other faiths can at all rival the glory of the good news of Jesus. The congregation warmed increasingly as they heard talks on the uniqueness of Jesus in our pluralist postmodern world and were taken on a whistle-stop tour of countries overseas where the church is growing abundantly. Stories of huge congregations in Latin America, Africa, Indonesia and China particularly impressed. We are not living in a post-Christian era after all – despite the impression which is constantly conveyed through the anti-Christian bias of much of the media.

On the Sunday morning the sermon expounded the call of the first four disciples in Matthew 4:18–22. Jesus' command is so simple. The disciples were called to 'come' and to 'follow' him – two very common words which we use easily in ordinary everyday conversation. Discipleship, we learned, means that we should *come* and keep coming to Jesus, forming an ever-closer relationship with him and growing in love for him. Then we are also called to *follow* Jesus in obedience as our Lord, to model our lives on him in his loving holiness and relationships, in his dreams and ambitions, in his concern for people's salvation – indeed in every aspect of his life and work.

The call of those first disciples continues with another vitally important, but very simple, easily understood word.

'And' is used to connect two inseparable concepts. The call to come to Jesus and follow him must never be separated from his determination to make us 'fishers of men and women'. In making us into his disciples, he sends us out into the oceans of the world to catch new fish, not just to keep aquariums in our comfortable Christian fellowships. Of course it is good to ensure that our aquariums remain healthy with a good flow of oxygen. The fish in the tank need regular feeding. It is pleasant too to beautify the tank with all sorts of ornaments and greenery. But the call on Jesus' disciples remains primarily to become fishermen. If no new fish are added to our collection, our present stock will gradually get older and eventually die out. Pastoral concern for the ongoing life of the church is vital, but without evangelistic witness and new people being added to our congregations, the church will die.

At this stage in the sermon I changed the metaphor. With due apologies I said to the congregation that I would like to tell them a very simple story. Although it might remind them of a biblical story, I stressed that this would be a new story of my own making. I told them of a shepherd who had a hundred sheep. In the evening he decided to bring all the sheep he had into the sheepfold, in case they were killed by the wild animals out on the mountainside. As he gathered them into the sheepfold, he began to count them. One – two – three – four – five – six . . . The congregation began to look anxious that I was going to count to ninety-nine!

But my story relates to the situation in Britain today. It gives a British contextualization to the story of the lost sheep in Matthew 18 and Luke 15. It is reckoned that a mere 6% of our population is meaningfully part of the Christian church.

In my story the shepherd occupies himself totally with the needs of his six sheep. They have to be fed regularly and it takes some hours to prepare their food. Combing their wool and ensuring that it remains clean further fills his time. The walls of the sheepfold need constant repair and attractive decoration. And the administration for six sheep is phenomenal! So, sadly our shepherd has neither the time nor the vision to go out into the mountains to search for his ninety-four lost sheep. They will be devoured by the savage wolves and will duly perish. As Christians today, we should be moved in our hearts as we see the great majority of our people rejecting or disregarding the Saviour.

Observing the fate of the lost sheep, the angels in heaven cannot rejoice before the Lord (cf. Luke 15:10). The angels' wings hang limply down in dejection!

That Sunday morning the Holy Spirit spoke powerfully to the vicar and the whole congregation. Together they knew God was calling them to a new outgoing mission in their neighbourhood. Every evening after dark in the city centre around the church, crowds of young people would gather in a drunken exchange of drugs and violence. Those Christians have now restructured their church to form a café in one aisle which is light and welcoming. A covered walkway encourages people to come off the streets into the warmth of the building for coffee, tea and refreshments. In the daytime too there is a stream of people coming into the church where they are warmly welcomed. Church members enjoy the opportunities for witness when visitors are not watching a Christian DVD.

One simple little story has been the Holy Spirit's means to transform that church. The whole atmosphere of the congregation changed radically. A new vision for local mission has captured their hearts.

Stories like this have more power than ever before in our society, because in Britain today postmodernism has captured our patterns of thought and communication. In postmodernism, people are reacting against a more traditional emphasis on objective and rational truth. So stories fit their way of thinking. Likewise, Eastern religions tend to be quite existentialist, with a strong emphasis on feelings rather than abstract reasoning. They have also gained enormous influence through the practice of yoga and Eastern meditation. These outworkings of Hinduism and Buddhism are now even available through the UK's National Health Service, and advertisements for them frequently adorn hospital notice-boards. In the existentialist context of both postmodernism and Eastern religions, storytelling fits well.

A story can change a person

'Would you be willing to come to our school and help our sixth-formers to understand Islam better?' My teacher friend had found herself having to teach about other faiths, and had done her best to read up about them. But she had never lived in a Muslim area or country and had not had the opportunity of learning first-hand. Books can give something of the theory, but a faith is always bigger than the formulations of a book.

We had some time to chat together before the class was due to begin. We wandered into the teachers' common room. Newspapers and magazines were scattered all over the tables and on one or two of the chairs. Dirty coffee mugs were littered around. But there was a feeling of comfortable infor-mality. A couple of other teachers were relaxing in refreshing silence. As we entered the room, one of them gave me a particularly warm smile of welcome. Quickly he came over to us and said how delighted he was to see me again. I felt somewhat embarrassed as I had no memory of him at all. Even his face looked totally unfamiliar to me.

'Remind me where we last met,' I ventured in the hope that his answer would jog my memory. To my surprise he replied, 'Twenty years ago when I was a student you spoke at the Bangor University Christian Union.' I smiled inwardly at his assumption that I would remember him! But I was impressed when he continued, 'You told us two stories from the time when you and your wife were missionaries in Indonesia.' He then proceeded to tell me what passage of Scripture I had expounded and what my main points had been. What a memory! Even stories from a far-off country like Indonesia could be used by God to influence someone's life in Britain. How much more might a more immediately relevant story change someone's life! This experience locally here in England reminded me that stories do not relate only in Asia, although that was where I had taken my first faltering footsteps in the practice of storytelling. People love and remember stories also in modern Europe.

He then reminded me what stories I had recounted. Stories have a wonderful way of sticking in people's memories and continuing over the years as God's instrument for speaking into our lives.

One of the stories was about a time when we were seriously short of water in the dry season. The town pump had broken down, the little local river dried up, and 20,000 people urgently needed water. As our containers began to run dry, we became desperate. Without water to wash the floors, fleas would hop unopposed into our home. And how could we deal with our baby's nappies and the mass of washing a child brings? Finally my wife and I agreed that she and our baby would go down to the big city of Medan and stay with friends there if no rain fell within the next twenty-four hours. Much prayer followed, although our faith could hardly stretch to imagine God sending rain in the middle of the dry season. But in his grace God answered miraculously. The next morning a major thunderstorm hit our town, and the fierce tropical rain was enough to fill every receptacle we possessed.

'Wasn't that rainstorm amazing?' I exclaimed to people the next day as they came to our town with their fruit and vegetables for market day.

'We didn't have any rain in our village,' one after another told us.

We later discovered that it had only rained on our town where water was so badly needed. You could go one mile in any direction and the surrounding villages missed the rainstorm.

For twenty years this story had remained firmly in the mind of that teacher. The point in my talk which the story illustrated had long been forgotten, but the story remained vividly in his memory. God had spoken to him through it. He had gained a new confidence that God's gracious kindness reaches out to us in whatever need we may experience – even when we may lack the faith to expect a miracle from God.

Having retold that story, he then proceeded to tell me the other story I had given in my talk all those years ago. One of the local Christian young people saw another lad, a violent gangster, on the street in our town in North Sumatra. Shaking with fear, he recalled the teenager's vicious violence, and began to run away as fast as he could. But the other lad called out to him, 'Don't be afraid, I'm a Christian now. My days of violence are in the past.' Jesus had met him and changed his life. He was now a fine Christian young man, and became a key leader in our local youth work. After this encounter the two lads had become firm friends and shared the gospel together in our town. In fact, they gained a strong reputation for their dynamic and open witness for Jesus. One of the young men who became a Christian through them came from a different ethnic group which at that time was entirely Muslim. The good news of Jesus had never before reached his area or people in Sumatra. Still a secondary school student, he returned to his Muslim village for the school holidays, witnessed about the good news of Jesus – and the Holy Spirit worked wonderfully. About a hundred people turned to the Lord and were baptized as Christians, the very first Christians in that whole area.[1] They looked to our young student friend as their church leader. Although he himself was just a new believer, he found himself in the position of having to run this new ex-Muslim church and be their Bible teacher.

'When I heard your stories, I knew that God was calling me to follow him and serve him with all I have and am,' our teacher friend shared. 'Those stories convinced me that I could trust God and that he wanted me to serve him for the rest of my life. As a school teacher I too want to live for Jesus and share his good news with the students here.' Two simple stories from a far-off country changed the whole course of his life. I realized again the powerful effect stories can have in people's lives – even when the storyteller is very ordinary.

Stories can change a person. Hopefully God had also spoken through the Bible teaching, but it was through the stories that the Spirit had really worked. My ordinary Bible exposition and teaching had long since been forgotten, but these simple stories remained vividly in this man's memory and were proving fruitful in his life even many years later. And despite my weakness, I was encouraged to realize that the fruit God gave through those stories had lasted (John 15:16). It was no flash in the pan.

Question:

- Has some biblical or other story impacted your life in a special way? If so, try to find an opportunity of telling that story to someone else. You could start by telling it to someone in your family or to some friends.

1. THE FIRST CHALLENGE

The little Saiburi harbour in South Thailand snuggled peace-fully in the darkness as the stickily hot sun gave way to the glory of the huge tropical moon. The long, elegant fishing boats with their outboard motors rested quietly in the shelter of the port's stone wall. Dr Gordon Gray and I knew that in the light of day the boats would display brightly painted sides with particular shapes and designs. A special Muslim shaman claimed the spiritual gift of determining the particular occult design which was ordained for each boat, but we had never been able to penetrate the wall of dark secrecy which lay concealed behind the boats and their attractively colourful decoration. When I had asked the shaman about the painting of one new boat with which he was involved, he had quickly changed the subject and all conversation immediately dried up.

The moon cut a swathe of light across the dark waters of the China Sea, and the rows of palms beyond the port stood out as silhouettes against the almost orange moon. Their

fronds swayed and rustled gently as the faintest of breezes
fanned the air, which still maintained something of the day's
stifling heat. But the ocean rested like a millpond, stretching
out darkly towards the east. Nevertheless, a regular chain of
minute waves lapped the sandy water's edge, adding their
peaceful music to the whole atmosphere.

It was in this context of soft beauty that Gordon Gray and
I strolled contentedly along the seashore. In those days before
air-conditioning, the relative cool of the evening came as a
relief at the end of a busy day's work in the hospital. As a fairly
new missionary I felt deeply privileged when Gordon invited
me to walk with him that evening. I was excited at the prospect
of having time with him all on my own. What would we talk
about? I had so much to learn from Gordon and was eager to
take on board anything he would share with me from his rich
years of experience. Yet I never realized that what he said
would influence me for the rest of my life. I certainly never
thought that it would inspire me to write a book on the
subject! My interest at that time in my life rested exclusively
on the work of mission in South Thailand. But later I was to
discover how Gordon's advice to me that evening would also
relate to witness in Britain and other countries.

With the onset of globalization, almost every place has
become fascinatingly multi-ethnic and multicultural. In Britain
this process began back in the 1960s and 1970s. The Beatles
started the fashion of following Indian gurus and introducing
Western forms of Asian religions. Fifty years later, Britain
has not only absorbed multitudes of Asian people with their
background cultures, but their Eastern religious patterns of
thought and communication have also infiltrated into the very
heart of British life. Asian patterns of telling stories are now
useful in communicating the Christian faith in Britain and the
rest of Europe.

Gordon Gray was known throughout the region for his brilliance as a doctor and surgeon. His fame in that area was particularly enhanced through various skull operations. The hospital received several patients whose skulls had been split open by falling *durians*, a large local fruit with a thick hard skin covered in fierce arrow-like thorns. When walking through a durian orchard, it was vitally important to avoid being directly under a tree in case a heavy over-ripe fruit, the size of a rugby ball, fell on your head. In the durian season the whole countryside was filled with the pungent odour of this amazing fruit, whose smell resembles a noxious mixture of rotten eggs and an unflushed lavatory plus any other strongly unpleasant odour you might imagine!

On one unforgettable occasion, a young woman came to the mission hospital after an accident with her fishing boat's outboard motor. Her long hair had got caught up in the propeller. Its swirling blades had ripped off the top of her scalp.

'What is your problem?' the nurse had asked her on her arrival at the Outpatients Department. In answer she said nothing, but quietly lifted the severed scalp off the top of her head. The nurse on duty nearly fainted in horror. Could anything be done to help her after such a terrible accident? Gordon Gray was called immediately, and operated on her with complete success. No wonder his fame spread throughout the region and people were heartfelt in their gratitude. They knew they were very privileged to have such a doctor in the mission hospital which they considered to be *their* hospital.

Local people often told me, with voices filled with admiration, that Gordon spoke both the Malay language and Thai absolutely perfectly. When people heard him talking, but could not see his white skin, they were convinced that he was a local man.

It was always a special joy when he was able to free himself from his medical calls to share in our daily hospital ward services. He would play his piano accordion, joining in with us in singing Christian songs. And then the patients would listen with rapt attention as he told biblical stories about the prophets and Old Testament characters whose names were known to our Muslim friends. They particularly loved his vivid renderings of the New Testament stories of Jesus. Gordon's warm friendliness and open humour won people's hearts as his humble smile made them feel at ease. Hearing the gospel clearly and directly from Gordon himself added considerable weight and credibility to what we said. As we witnessed from bed to bed among the inpatients and from person to person in the outpatient queues, we could feel the significance of Gordon's witness for Jesus.

I had only been living and working as a missionary in Asia for about a year, and language study still played a major role in my life as I grappled with the local Malay dialect. Despite my inexperience our leaders had asked me to work as the hospital evangelist among the Malay people, who were Muslim and largely unevangelized.

The indigenous population in the provinces of South Thailand were almost entirely Malay and Muslim, but the towns were occupied by Thai Buddhist business people and district officials. They of course spoke Thai. There was also a sprinkling of Chinese people who ran businesses and small wayside cafés. They spoke a wide variety of Chinese languages, so the area resounded with a rich multitude of languages. In the mission hospital, I worked together with Minka Hanskamp, a slightly older and more experienced Dutch woman who was responsible for working with Thai-speaking patients. Each morning Minka and I met for prayer together, asking that God would work by his Spirit and bring Malay and Thai patients to a committed faith in Jesus.

Later Minka was sadly taken captive by extremist Muslim rebels, based in the jungle-clad mountains, who were fighting for independence. Most of the Muslim population were warmly friendly and by no means religiously fanatical or violent. But this small minority in the mountains spread danger and uncertainty throughout the region. As our mission held firmly to its policy of never paying bribes or ransoms, there was little hope for Minka's life. Tragically, she was held for nearly a year and then martyred. Her grave in Saiburi next to the old hospital still reminds us today of the challenge of willing sacrifice in mission for Jesus Christ.

I cannot remember what Gordon and I talked about on our pleasant stroll in the relative cool of that evening. But one sentence still stands out vividly in my memory: 'If we want to communicate effectively with Malay Muslims, we shall have to learn to tell stories.'

His words struck home as if God had spoken directly to me with an audible voice. I knew that I was being called to change the whole format of my witness and preaching. Since then, I have gained some experience in using stories among Muslims. When I returned to Britain, I discovered that here too story-telling is enormously effective among Muslims. Then I came gradually to realize that the practice of storytelling is useful in all our Christian witness and in teaching the good news of Jesus in every continent, culture and religious background. God speaks through stories, and people often remember stories for many years. Children, of course, love to snuggle into the loving arms of a parent or other relative or friend on the sofa while they listen to a story. But we all enjoy an interesting story.

In this book I plan to share some of what God has graciously taught me about telling stories, not only in Asia, but also in

Britain and in other very different contexts around the world. And what fun it is to communicate the good news of Jesus through stories! I hope and pray that readers of this book will gain the courage to start telling stories – perhaps at first in the safety of our own home with those we know and trust, but then more widely with friends, neighbours and people we work with.

Question:

- Has anything someone else said to you changed the course of your life in some way? Pray that God will use something you say to set someone else's feet on a new path of loving and serving the Lord.

2. TELLING STORIES AND INFLUENCING MINDS

Up and down the country, people watched another tragic story on their televisions – the struggle of a man with an incurable and painful illness. He could no longer do anything at all for himself, and in his absolute impotence felt like an intolerable burden on his wife and family. Personal dignity had long since evaporated. In even the most basic things – eating, washing, going to the toilet, using a handkerchief when coughing or sneezing – he was utterly dependent on his carers. There was not the slightest hope of any alleviation of his suffering, let alone a cure. There seemed to be no light at the end of the tunnel except the relief of death.

The programme pointed out that this man longed to die, but his desire for death was frustrated by the law which at present forbids euthanasia. Even if he could persuade his wife or his doctor to administer some injection to bring about his death, this was illegal and they would be guilty of murder. The only possibility seemed to lie in going all the way to

Switzerland, a more tolerant and sympathetic country where euthanasia has been legalized. He could then visit a clinic which specializes in helping people like him to bring an end to their lives. But in his condition the journey to Switzerland was no simple matter. How would he manage the flight with all his disabilities? And financially could he and his family afford it? The television programme implied that it is unjust that only wealthier families can manage the expense of travelling to another country, where euthanasia is possible.

Such stories move people's hearts, but the strong arguments against legalized euthanasia are seldom mentioned in such programmes.

This is a fictitious case, unrelated to any similar story on TV news. But from time to time we see stories of this nature on TV and the implications are clear – we are made to feel that the law on euthanasia needs to be altered. As we watch, we find ourselves naturally sympathizing with the fearful suffering of the terminally ill patient. Any sensitive or loving person will long for some relief to be made possible for them. One's heart goes out too to the family members who share their loved one's agony and as full-time carers may find their own lives severely restricted.

Such agonizing stories play a vital part in forming people's views on many an ethical problem. In a democracy a groundswell of public opinion has a significant influence on our lawmakers in parliament. Indeed the political debate on such topics is often based on such extreme, heart-rending stories. One such story can sway public opinion and stop people even considering an alternative view.

As Christians we also need to learn to move people's hearts and minds through telling the story of one particular person in such a way that it tugs at people's heart strings. Of course our story will need to be backed up by rational argument and biblical teaching, but we aim to move hearts as well as minds. Christian organizations involved in care for the needy already practise this, as do Christian ecological and environmental movements. But evangelistic and church missions may still have much to learn in this.

'Soaps' and other drama programmes on television and radio are also used to inform and form public opinion. Useful teaching can be imparted through the portrayal of the various characters and the storyline. So, for example, from its outset the radio series *The Archers* set out to convey practical teaching on aspects of village life, health issues and encouragement to grow your own produce.

Thanks partly to the influence of stories in the media, drink-driving has become unacceptable to most people. Tales of the danger of drugs have also been told – but sadly this has failed to penetrate deeply into people's minds. Sometimes stories depicting health issues or ecological matters are aired, percolating into our consciousness. On the negative side, angry words and unhappy relationships have been shown in dramas as a normal part of life. Does this just reflect the realities of contemporary society or is it actually forming people's behaviour?

Of course popular thinking, political debate and the making of law must not only depend on such cases. Statistical research, for instance, should also be used to support an argument.

For example, the euthanasia debate needs rational discussion about its rights and wrongs as well as clear-thinking argument concerning the consequences of a change in the law. How would it affect other frail old people? Would it expose them to undue pressure from greedy relatives who might be waiting to inherit and may therefore put pressure on the old person to hasten his or her death? Many old people are tempted to feel that they are useless and therefore could in a moment of weakness or depression prematurely sign away their life. And thought must also be given to the fearful pressures which members of the medical profession would face if they had to determine whether it was right to hasten death by euthanasia. The forming of law must never depend only on individual stories.

Nevertheless, in our postmodern world stories play a major part in forming people's opinions – including in parliament. This is true even when rational debate joins forces with the more subjective influence of personal stories. Christians in everyday witness need to get in on the act.

We have given the example of how a story can be used by the media to change people's beliefs concerning euthanasia. The same is equally true for the debate on same-sex relationships and abortion. In its strong support for equal rights for same-sex couples the media often introduces the story of a loving, faithful couple whose experience will win the approval of all who watch or read. It will not tell of same-sex couples whose relationship is torn apart unhappily. The media will not mention that the statistics for the breakdown of same-sex unions are even worse than for divorce among heterosexual married couples. The media also never informs the public concerning the medical problems associated with homosexual sexual union or the grave dangers of legalizing euthanasia.

Likewise with abortion it is stories of young women in desperate need which are told in order to move our hearts and push us into supporting a lax approach to the subject: not those who get rid of a baby for their own convenience. It may even be considered unacceptable to discuss publicly the medical and psychological consequences of having an abortion.

As with euthanasia, so also with other issues such as abortion and same-sex couples' rights it is *stories* that play a leading role in forming public opinion and therefore influencing our lawmakers. As Christians we will do well to add a live story of an actual situation to our more theoretical arguments. We need to learn in our evangelism and Christian teaching to make more use of stories, for it is often these which move people's hearts and minds. Like the media, we should not be afraid to use quite emotive stories – but we should be careful not to manipulate people through exerting excessive emotional pressure. As witnesses to Christian values which alone can bring true happiness and love, we long for our message to win the hearts and minds of our nation.

Jesus himself did much of his teaching through short, snappy stories from everyday life. For example, he told of a woman with ten coins. She lost one. She didn't just rejoice in the remaining nine, but searched everywhere until she had recovered the lost coin. Such a story brings home to us God's call to witness and evangelism in a much more pertinent way than an abstract exhortation to witness. Plain biblical teaching without stories can become somewhat dull and uninspiring without living stories to enliven it.

As Christians we long for the good news of Jesus to grip people's minds and hearts, bringing a new popular movement towards the Lord and his church. This may come about more easily if we capture their attention through personal stories. The example of the media and of our politicians should move us to try declaring our faith through such emotionally gripping stories. This must affect our understanding of Christian truth and the way we express our beliefs to those around us.

God works through stories

'Che' Sof! Che' Sof!' I heard the Malay man's cry across the hall in Saiburi, South Thailand. But it didn't occur to me that it had anything to do with me. I was visiting some twenty years after I had worked there and had forgotten the Malay name people had given me. Somehow the local form of 'Mr Joseph' had felt fitting.

The man rushed across the hall and greeted me warmly as a long-lost friend, but I had no idea who he was.

'You came to my village years ago and told us the story of Jesus,' he exclaimed excitedly. 'You even showed us how the stories of Jesus fit into how Allah created the world, how Adam and Eve fell into sin and what Allah was doing in this world century after century.' He beamed at me and told us how he had turned from Islam and become a follower of Jesus. 'It all made such good sense,' he continued, 'and I couldn't get all those stories out of my mind. So finally after quite a struggle I gave my life to Jesus and received his salvation.' As we talked further, he shared how in Islam he could never work out how the world moved on from creation to the coming of one prophet after another. But the story of the Bible with its climax in Jesus Christ had captured his heart.

During my short time of service in Thailand I had not known of any Muslim becoming a Christian, so his story all those years later was deeply encouraging. But I realized that he was the only Christian in an area full of Muslim villages. Through the Bible story, with its message of salvation through Jesus' death and resurrection, this Muslim man had not only been converted, but also kept safe as a follower of Jesus for twenty years despite constant pressure to return to Islam.

But Gordon Gray's advice to tell stories is true not only for South Thailand, but also for the West today. Storytelling has become such a major element in contemporary communication that people have even invented a new word – 'storying'. As Christians in our world of existentialism and postmodernism, with their emphasis on what is actually happening now rather than rational arguments, it is vitally important that we learn to tell compelling stories if we want our views to be heard. A purely rational debate will no longer win the day. An objective presentation of truth may sound both somewhat boring and also old-fashioned and out of touch with the modern world. We live in an era which is deeply suspicious of rational argument and even of scientific truth. Subjective stories not only hold people's attention more easily, but they are also the culturally accepted method of communication. If we want to relate to our contemporary culture and society, we shall have to listen to Dr Gordon Gray's advice.

Narrative theology

In this chapter we shall be looking at how our Christian theology and our basic beliefs are shaped by an underlying story. So often in the past, stories have been thought fit only for children in Sunday schools, while expressions of an adult Christian faith should be abstract and theoretical. For example, no serious theological book could teach Christian truth through stories. No academic thesis could be presented with stories as its main content. As a result, there is a danger that for some people the very word 'theology' implies lifelessly dull and boring theory. Contemporary narrative theology has begun to bring theology and biblical commentary to life again. It is of course vitally important for the whole future of the Christian faith and church that its teachings should be dynamic and alive. Narrative and stories lie at the heart of this struggle.

Storytelling is also pragmatically effective in the communication of the good news of Jesus. Through stories we can win attention and give our message wide circulation and acceptance. Already in South Thailand I observed how people not only enjoyed my stories and listened with rapt attention to them, but also often went home afterwards to their housing area or village and told them to their families and friends. In this way stories related to the gospel spread more widely to people I would never have met. And surely local men and women told my stories much better than I did – they were probably more gifted than me at telling stories and they certainly knew the language much better. In Britain too, people go home after hearing a story being told and say to their family, 'Such an interesting thing happened to me today. I was in the office and one of the salespeople told us a really unusual story.' They may then retell it.

But the telling of stories is not only a pragmatic issue or a question of cultural adaptation in cross-cultural mission. In the history of the Christian church, biographies have always been highly significant in shaping Christians' spiritual lives. Already in the first centuries of the Christian church, stories about the great heroes of the Bible inspired Christians' love for the Lord. And the experiences of Anthony and other Egyptian desert fathers joined with tales from the Syrian desert and biographies such as Augustine's *Confessions*. In later centuries Christians were deeply influenced both in the practice of their faith and in their beliefs by the stories of courageous modern missionaries as well as the great 'saints'. The biographies of historical figures like Augustine, Bernard of Clairvaux or Francis of Assisi have inspired Christians throughout the centuries.

We too can usefully tell stories of up-to-date Christians and people we personally know. It can also be very moving and instructive when we recount our own experiences as Christians. Of course our friends and associates will love to hear how we first became believers in Jesus and what this meant in our lives. But our personal stories should go beyond that and tell of how God has worked in our lives, answers to prayer, God's faithfulness even when we fail him, how we have dealt with temptation, suffering or difficulties in life. This can play a vital part in our witness.

'Could I buy your and your wife's life stories, please? I always enjoy people's personal stories.' Such words are frequently said to me when I display our books for sale after speaking in a church. People appreciate relevant stories of contemporary life. We also find that more people tell us of special blessing in their lives through our biographies than through our other books. God uses personal stories very particularly.

In modern times, theologians have begun to regain this emphasis on stories. So-called narrative theology has gained centre stage both in the ivory towers of academic theology and in more popular expressions of a biblical Christian faith. Narrative theology is based on the fact that God reveals himself and his will in stories, not just in stark doctrinal formulations. Our beliefs are based upon the narrative of Scripture. This shift of emphasis from a more theoretical view of the Christian faith may open the door for the message of the Lord to become more relevant and attractive in today's Europe.

Our creeds, from Nicaea and Chalcedon, only contain bare statements of fact, but the Bible's method of stating our faith is by telling the story of events where God has blessed his people.

So Stephen declares his faith in his final message by listing what God has done for Israel from the call of Abraham onwards (Acts 7). In this way he also turns the tables and shows the sin of those who were accusing him of blasphemy. His self-defence consists of biblical stories, not some abstract theological statement.

As Christians we are constantly faced with the question of biblical interpretation. The Bible consists, of course, of a large library of very diverse books and we all need a way to approach it.

Ever since the Enlightenment movement swept through the Western world, we have tended to interpret the Bible with rationalistic doctrinal eyes rather than also underlining our spiritual feelings and loving relationships with the Lord.

'What does this book of the Bible reveal concerning the central doctrines of the Christian faith as expressed in the early church creeds and in our theological studies?' Christian leaders have often asked such questions as they have sought to interpret and understand God's revelation in the Bible.

Not only biblical interpretation, but also theology has reflected this approach. However, such rational and cognitive approaches have come under severe scrutiny in our present age of existentialism and now of postmodernism. The systematized and scientific understanding of our faith has been widely rejected in favour of a more existential and experiential key to biblical theology. The search for truth has yielded very considerably to the hunger for existential experience. Not only in high-flown theological thinking, but also in our everyday Christian faith we are all emphasizing the overall sweep of the biblical story more than a traditional theoretical theology or catalogue of truths. It is vitally important that our Christian faith and our witness should fit our contemporary culture.

Thus in conversation an agnostic London businessman reacted to me with surprise when the word 'truth' was used. 'Truth!' he exclaimed. 'I don't think I've heard that word since I was a boy.' He then added, 'After all, no-one believes in truth nowadays, do they?' As biblical Christians we do believe, however, that Jesus is not only the way and the life, but also the truth (John 14:6). Following the story of the woman caught in adultery, Jesus teaches that 'the truth will set you free' (John 8:32). The existential story goes hand in hand with truth. It must convey and portray truth, but it must do so in stories and word-pictures as well as doctrinal statements.

Various theologians have therefore concentrated on the fundamental story of Scripture as the basis for their teaching of the truth. N. T. Wright, the former Bishop of Durham, is one example. His writings have particular influence and popularity because of his brilliant ability to publish both significant theological works of academic depth and also more popular, smaller biblical commentaries and other easier books. This combination of the academic and the popular approach means that his biblical and theological insights gain credibility and wide acceptance. It is a model which we all need to emulate as best we can. We too in our faith and witness need his combination of profound biblical and theological truth with a lively storytelling approach.

N. T. Wright emphasizes the reality of an underlying story which runs through the whole of the biblical revelation like a golden thread. This story forms the content of what God is doing in the world and wants to do in the lives of his people. No radical break separates the New Testament from its Old Testament roots, for the New Testament is picking up on the same Old Testament story and developing it more fully.

This emphasis on the oneness of the Old and New Testaments may particularly be seen in the way that the life of Jesus to a considerable extent parallels the story of Israel, from the exodus from Egypt through to the entry into Canaan, from Israel's exile in Babylon to its return to the Promised Land, as we will see below. Indeed the early Christians were known as people of 'the Way' (*hodos* in Greek). Thus the history of the church also picks up on the same story of the exodus (*ex-hodos*) and the return from exile. Wright asserts that at the time of Jesus the Jews were deeply aware that they were still living in a time of exile. This was under-lined by the harsh realities of Roman occupation. Although Jesus did not come to deliver his people from Roman political and military oppression, as the Messiah he does deliver from sin – his name is 'Jesus' (Saviour) (Matthew 1:21).

The history of Israel, with its judges and kings, seems doomed throughout to end in the exile to Babylon. From then on, the final destruction of Jerusalem by the Romans seems a foregone conclusion. But each tragic event of exile ends with God's wonderful work of salvation. First came the great event of the Passover, when God brought his people out of slavery into the Promised Land, a land of milk and honey. Then came the return to Israel after the seventy years of exile in Babylon. And the climax comes with the story of the Messiah Jesus himself, whose life moves with fixed determin-ation to its fearful conclusion, his death on the cross. But the suffering of Jesus' atoning work on the cross gives way to the glorious reality of the resurrection and ascension. So Jesus stands as the final fulfilment of the long biblical history of exile and suffering, release and salvation. In and through Jesus, God saves his people from their sin and gives them the fullness of new life. Tom Wright sees that the whole revelation of the Bible and of Christian teaching circles around this story of exile and God's gracious salvation from that exile.

The golden thread of the one biblical narrative may be seen in the fact that the story and history of the people of Israel in the Old Testament is continued and developed through the life, death, resurrection and ascension of Jesus. It then continues into the story of the growing Christian church. Whether in Sunday school teaching or with adults, it may be helpful to give a quick bird's-eye view of the narrative of biblical history, so that the various well-known biblical stories fit into place within this scheme of exile and salvation. The overall story of God in action through the history of Israel and the church will prove richly instructive in our own personal Christian life and in sharing our faith with others. Ordinary Christians may also be able to apply this overall biblical story in our personal witness. Perhaps God has led us through some particular suffering, but has delivered. For example, an elderly friend of ours became blind and physically very weak, while his wife was clearly dying in hospital. In God's wonderful goodness, both of them died within twenty-four hours of each other, and neither of them knew that the lifelong marriage partner had also died. Death and entry into eternal life can also be God's glorious deliverance from suffering.

Jewish Christians find it particularly significant that *ekklesia*, the Greek word for the church, was used in the Septuagint, the Greek translation of the Old Testament, for the *congregation* of Israel. In passing, we may smile therefore at the error of the common glib affirmation that Pentecost was the birthday of the church. The church is the congregation of Israel together now with new non-Jewish believers, the international church of Jesus the Messiah. The birth of the *ekklesia*, the congregation of Israel, took place long before Pentecost! Perhaps at the birth of 'our father' Abraham? Or perhaps even further back in the creation of Adam and Eve, our natural ancestors?

Paul shows this clearly in Romans 11. The olive tree of Israel may lose some (not all) of its natural Jewish branches through their unbelief. Then some unnatural non-Jewish branches are added to that same tree of Israel, and finally the multitude of natural Jewish branches will be re-grafted back into their tree. The story of Israel continues even to the eschatological end, but it no longer remains exclusive or particularistic. So the Old Testament story widens out in the

New Testament to include not only Jews, but also people of every nation and people. This great truth is fundamental to our Christian mission not only among Jews, but with all people. As Christians we are called to share our faith with those in our midst who are not ethnically British and who follow other religions. The church should no longer be entirely white, but should also include people of every colour and religious background. This is particularly true for Christians in our universities and colleges where overseas students abound. And we shall find that overseas students and people from an ethnic minority background will very much appreciate witness and teaching which comes through stories.

We notice again how God's revelation in the New Testament develops naturally from its roots in the Old Testament. The whole Bible is one continuous story, into which we now fit as its spiritual descendants.

Understanding and teaching the Bible with a golden-thread story

We have noted how N. T. Wright and others have pointed out that the New Testament story of Jesus and the early church develops in line with the underlying truths of Israel's slavery in Egypt, Passover, exodus and wanderings through the desert to the Promised Land. Parallel to this narrative, Israel's exile in Babylon and its return to the land undergirds the New Testament writings. Now we ask how this pattern can help us in our biblical teaching in our churches, in our own personal walk with the Lord and in our witness as Christians.

Pastors, Bible teachers, youth and children's workers should be asking what particular needs and situations their people are facing. How does the Bible relate to those needs? If so, how can we use its underlying story to draw out the relevant teaching of the Bible? Matthew's Gospel lends itself ideally to this sort of teaching.[2]

In his popular books of Bible exposition, N. T. Wright starts each chapter with a story which forms the background to the passage of Scripture he is writing about. This story helps the reader to understand the meaning of the passage. I like to expound and teach Matthew's Gospel with the illustrative backdrop of the traditional English story of the mother watching her soldier son drilling on the parade ground. As he marched up and down with his platoon, his mother proudly pointed out to the woman standing next to her: 'Look, my son is the only soldier in step!' Everyone laughs at such stupidity, but I then point out that the mother was right! The sergeant major was ordering 'Right, right, right', and all the soldiers except her son had their right foot forwards. But actually the sergeant major was wrong. He should have been ordering 'Left, left, left', and all the other soldiers were therefore wrong to obey him with their right foot forwards. Although the mother's son was out of step with his officer and all the other soldiers, he was actually the only one who was right.

It is hard to face the position where one has to be the only soldier in step. But in Britain and many of our European countries we face exactly this situation. When we go home from church, we may well be the only practising Christian in our block of flats or street. Each of our young people will very likely be the only committed Christian in their class. Their teacher may also oppose their Christian faith. Young people and children always like to be part of a group of friends, so it is doubly hard for them to be the only soldier in step with the Christian faith. Our teaching must relate to this situation and we may want to use the story of the soldier's proud mother and Matthew's Gospel ourselves.

Matthew was writing to a remnant Jewish church in just such a situation, so his Gospel is particularly relevant to us in Europe where Christians are a very small and uninfluential part of our society. In Matthew's day the rabbis, political leaders and key people were very probably all against Jesus as Messiah. Those first-century Jewish believers in Jesus must have felt very alone. They must have wondered sometimes whether they had made a bad mistake in following Jesus when all the brilliant leaders of their people stood strongly against him. They will have felt the enormous difficulty of holding true to their faith in Jesus, of being the only soldiers in step. Likewise in Britain today, media personalities, so-called 'celebrities' and other leaders in our society seem to stand against our faith, so Matthew and the church to which he was writing are still exceedingly relevant to us in our Christian life and witness.

Matthew therefore emphasizes that Jesus is so glorious that he is worth following even when we do so alone. It is not appropriate in this book to demonstrate how all of Matthew's Gospel is aimed at encouraging those few remnant believers to march with confidence as the only ones in step. But we can illustrate it with relevant stories in our application and teaching, thus making our expositions come alive with a vitally true application.

N. T. Wright as a narrative theologian

N. T. Wright gives us a model for the use of narrative and story when defining our faith. He is also perhaps the leading theological writer in Britain today, so it is important that we learn from him in our understanding and communication of Christian truth. His books are also very popular.

Wright describes the narrative story as a five-act drama. We may not be in a position to share our biblical faith with the brilliance of N. T. Wright, but in our experience of the work of Jesus in our lives we can enter into the drama of the biblical story. In our teaching and witness we can also help people to feel the glory of that story. All of us in our witness can recount the basic overall thread of the biblical story and apply it to whatever situations people are facing.

1. Creation

The foundation of everything in the Bible is the story of God's creation of the natural world and of humanity. Although there are no doctrinal definitions in the first chapters of Genesis, the story gives a clear picture of God himself. His purposes for the world and for humanity are revealed. From the creation account we may deduce God's ideals for his creation and for humanity.

While it remains true that God is in a particular way 'the God of Israel', he is shown in the creation story to be the one true God over all the earth. He created everything and everyone, so everything and everyone should belong to him. In the story of the creation it becomes evident that all peoples everywhere are descended from Adam and Eve. The Old Testament picks up on this theme by showing again and again how God controls the destinies of all nations and all creation. He shows his power over the wind and waves; he blesses or judges Gentile people and nations according to his own sense of justice and truth. As Creator, he is indeed 'Lord of all'. He is not only 'the God of Israel', but also Lord over all the earth – even over Britain!

In our society today, pluralism has become the accepted foundation for all religious thinking. It is assumed that different countries and their peoples each have their own particular faith. And all religions are considered to be equally valid for their followers, but none has universal truth for all people. So it is felt that Indians are Hindus, Arabs are Muslim, Jews are Judaistic, Thai are Buddhists, Latin Americans are Roman Catholic, and Africans follow their traditional tribal faiths. As soon as anyone examines this presupposition, it is obviously ridiculous. Each of these peoples holds to various faiths, including the Christian faith. It is in a situation just like this that the Bible asserts that the Creator God is sovereign over the whole world and demands allegiance from all. How relevant the Bible is to our current worldviews! Let us rejoice for ourselves and also witness accordingly as we grapple with the biblical revelation!

2. Crisis

No reader of the story of creation can fail to note the fearful contrast between God's ideals and the sad realities of our lives both individually and as societies and nations. The Garden of Eden stands in sharp contrast with the natural disasters of tsunamis, volcanic eruptions, earthquakes, droughts and floods. Genesis does not define theologically the ultimate cause or the current nature of sin and evil in the world, but the stories of the fall and of the development of early humanity in Genesis 3 – 11 imprint a clear impression on our thinking.

The consequences of the fall form the foundation for the whole message of Paul's letter to the Romans. In chapter 1 he shows how Gentiles wallow in moral and religious sin, so that they 'did not think it worth while to retain the knowledge of God' (Romans 1:28). So God actively 'gave them over in the sinful desires of their hearts' and 'to shameful lusts' (1:24, 26). How telling these descriptions sound to British ears today! Paul goes on in Romans 2:1–16 to widen the net to all who pass judgment on others and think themselves better than those around them. He concludes in 2:17 – 3:8 by showing that Jews equally '[break] the law' and so 'God's name is blasphemed among the Gentiles because of you'. All stand equally condemned as sinners.

Paul proves the reality of his assertion by reminding his readers of the stories of Abraham, the father of the people of Israel. In Genesis we may revel in the brilliant accounts of Abraham's call, God's covenant with him and his descendants, the promise of a child in his old age and the sacrifice of Isaac. But Genesis makes no attempt to formulate a conceptual theology from these stories. Even Paul's use of those stories falls far short of developing a systematic theological statement, although it does give us a profound understanding of truth. But the truth is based on the stories.

3. Community

The story of God's call of Abraham forms the foundation for the whole history of Israel as God's people in the Old Testament. God calls Abraham with the intention that he should become the father of a great nation. Indeed, God's purpose reaches out beyond the narrow confines of his natural descendants. Abraham was to be a blessing not only for Israel, but also so that 'all peoples on earth will be blessed through you' (Genesis 12:2–3).

We see in Romans how this Old Testament theme is developed in the New Testament. Paul underlines the aim of God that Abraham should be 'the father of many nations' (Romans 4:18), not just of Israel. In this way Paul is defending his call to preach the gospel not just among his own Jewish people, but particularly among the Gentiles in Spain (Romans 15:23–29). We may note here the call to international mission inherent in such biblical passages. We too are called to bear witness not only among our own people, but also to Jews and Gentiles of every nation and people.

God earnestly desires that humanity should live with close relationships within a community of righteous holiness and loving grace. It is through his covenant community that God achieves his purposes. So God calls his people to be 'holy as he is holy' (see 1 Peter 1:15) and reveals his law with the aim of moulding Israel into a community of holiness and loving unity. He would be their God and they would be his people. In this way Israel should be a model, to attract all peoples to faith in the living God and his Messiah.

God's purposes find their fulfilment through the congregation of Israel and the church. God longs for his people to display his righteousness, holiness and love. He gives them the law to show them how to reflect his nature of holiness. In the essential nature of God, the three persons of the Trinity are deeply one in love, so he calls his people to develop relationships like his own. They are to serve one another in a love and unity which parallels the life of the Trinity. If Israel could have achieved this ideal, the light of God would have shone out into the whole world. This call to Israel remains today a challenge for us all as individual Christians, and in our life and worship together as churches.

Although Paul's heart was primarily engaged with the task of mission to the Gentiles, he knew that God's mission is accomplished through the church community. So Paul also dedicates much of his energy to promoting our sanctification in the church. In our individualistic world we need to underline that followers of Jesus are born again into the great family of God. We belong to God's church and need to become vital members of it. Together as churches we are called to demonstrate the reality and beauty of the Lord.

The ultimate goal of God's mission through us in the church is that Israel and the surrounding nations might 'know that I am the Lord your God'. These often-repeated words form the conclusion of several key events in the story of the exodus from Egypt and the entry into the Promised Land. It is the events themselves which demonstrate that YHWH is indeed 'the Lord your God'.

4. Christ

The pinnacle of the biblical story is found in the glorious reality of Jesus the Messiah. The amazing historical truth of his birth outshines even the earlier Old Testament accounts of God coming down to this world. In Jesus, God himself breaks into history to transform the world and all humanity. What a story to tell the world!

The incarnation leads into the story of Jesus' life here on earth, revealing the perfect holiness which is God's purpose for us. We see the love and grace of God in the story of Jesus' utter sinlessness, his perfect relationships, his total obedience to the Father, his gracious love towards all sorts of people, his dynamic power in salvation from sin, sickness, storms and demonic possession. How well I remember a visitor to our home telling in brief a catalogue of Jesus' miracles one after another! It sounded exciting and we were all spellbound. None of us could fail to be awestruck at Jesus' gracious love and power. Our guest did not need to point to the moral; the stories conveyed the message wonderfully.

The story of Jesus in the Gospels always has in its sights the climax of his death and resurrection. Each of the Gospel writers gives a relatively large proportion of their story to the cross and resurrection as the ultimate purpose of Jesus' coming to earth.

The Gospel writers hardly mention the theological significance of the cross as God's means of atonement and redemption or of the resurrection which gives his followers the promise of new life. This may be implied, but it is not generally spelled out in direct theological terms. Traditionally, therefore, Christian preachers and teachers have underlined Mark 10:45 where it is stated that Jesus came 'to give his life as a ransom for many'. Here at least it is felt that the Gospels give us a clear theological statement, although the verse is really demonstrating that 'whoever wants to be first must be slave of all' (10:44).

While this verse does indeed affirm that Jesus gave his life as a sacrifice in order to redeem and ransom the multitudes of humanity, some Christians forget to look at this verse in its context. They can become so taken up with the theological truth of Jesus' atoning work in our place on the cross that they fail to notice the true significance of this verse. It comes in the context of James and John seeking the pre-eminent status and position of sitting in the places of honour at Jesus' right hand. Jesus counters their self-seeking desire by declaring that true greatness as his disciples lies in becoming humble servants: 'Whoever wants to be first must be slave of all.' In this upside-down view of Christian discipleship we follow in the footsteps of Jesus himself. He 'did not come to be served, but to serve, and to give his life as a ransom for many'. We may imagine that in the back of Jesus' mind he was contrasting the *giving* of his life with *receiving* people's gifts and esteem.

So we may observe that even Mark 10:45 in its context is not meant as a theological statement, but rather it is a very practical rebuke in the vivid story of two disciples following their natural desire for status and position. Jesus' disciples were not unique in seeking status for themselves! This story can easily be adapted to fit a modern context. We can picture two workers going to their manager and asking for special favours. You do not have to be a skilled storyteller to recount that sort of story.

5. The church

As we have already noted, the church in the New Testament is the continuation of the congregation of Israel. The church is also the body of Christ, continuing the life and work for which he came to earth, died and rose again.

In John 12 the coming of the Gentile Greeks to Jesus forms the climax to the whole life of Jesus and opens the door for the final act of the crucifixion and resurrection of Jesus. When those Gentiles came to him, Jesus excitedly exclaimed, 'The hour has come for the Son of Man to be glorified' (John 12:23), and he goes on to state that 'I, when I am lifted up from the earth, will draw all men to myself' (John 12:32).

In his death on the cross, Jesus opens the door for people of all nations and ethnic groups to come into a vital relationship with him. The way is now prepared, but the actual task of sharing this good news with the whole world remains. John's repeated emphasis on the words 'all', 'many' and 'much' reminds us of the universal task to which the church is called. John even starts his Gospel with the fact of creation. God created everyone and everything, so *all* should be following the divine Word. In John 1:9–10 he underlines the word 'world' by repeating it four times – in the New Testament merely repeating a word twice emphasizes it. To repeat a word four times in two sentences is the equivalent of using bold, italics and underlining!

Luke stresses the universal task of the Christian church. In the book of Acts we read the story of the early church's missionary outreach first to the Jews in Judea (Acts 1 – 7) and then also to the Gentiles, beginning with the conversion of Cornelius in Acts 10. The Spirit's work among the mixed-race Samaritans and the conversion of the Ethiopian eunuch on his way home from worshipping the God of Israel in Jerusalem form a bridge between the Jews and the Gentiles (Acts 8).

Then, as the introduction to Gentile mission, Luke gives us an account of the conversion of Paul, the apostle to the Gentiles (Acts 9).

Paul really starts his work of internationalizing the church by including the Gentiles in Acts 13, where he calls out to an angry Jewish crowd the bold and dramatic words, 'We now turn to the Gentiles' (Acts 13:46). From then on, he led the way in the church's outreach to Gentiles, thus opening the door for God's kingdom and church to spread to all nations. It should, however, be noted that his turning to the Gentiles did not mean that he no longer preached to his fellow Jews. Immediately after his 'turning to the Gentiles' in Antioch of Pisidia he 'went as usual into the Jewish synagogue' (Acts 14:1) and as a result 'a great number of Jews and Gentiles believed'.

The story of the church remains incomplete. The kingdom of God has come in the person of Jesus, the King of kings. Now in the post-resurrection era the kingdom is spreading all over the world to Jews and Gentiles, to people of every nation everywhere. But we still follow the Lord's Prayer and ask that his kingdom may come in its fullness, that his will may be done on earth just as it is in heaven. We wait eagerly for the finale, the perfect conclusion to the biblical story. The book of Acts is not just a nice storybook. Luke has definite axes to grind. He is using the story of the early church to teach us all what God's purposes are for the mission of his church, including his people in Britain and the West today. Our lives should be based on the underlying story of the Bible. This story is God's Word to us all today. It is also the basis of our witness to the world. In the book of Acts the account of the early church's witness by the power of the Spirit should inspire us to study the story of the outreach of the church through the centuries and share with our churches the exciting story of what God is doing today in other continents. Such stories will motivate us to play our part in the ongoing mission of the church.

Question:

- What stories could you use to teach about the glorious spread of God's kingdom in our world today?

3. STORIES IN OTHER FAITHS

'I've just led a Hindu girl to faith in Jesus. But I don't really know anything about her Hindu background, so could you just chat more with her and check that she has understood the gospel?' The pastor had preached an evangelistic sermon and given an appeal at the end, to which the Hindu girl had responded. She was still kneeling at the front of the church when I went over to her.

She nodded with enthusiasm as she heard again what Jesus had done for her. She was eager to receive his promised cleansing from her sin, his gift of full salvation and new resurrection life. She warmed too to the reality of the work of the Holy Spirit not only in helping her to live a better life, but also through his power to free her from all attacks by evil spirits. I began to share the pastor's joy in witnessing her salvation.

But then I asked a key question for any Hindu-background person wanting to come to faith in Jesus. Was she willing to put away all other gods and turn only to Jesus for salvation and eternal life? Or was she just adding Jesus and his salvation to her pantheon of gods, each of which would help her in one way or another?

She was horrified at the idea of only following one lord and having to forego all other deities. She was in no way willing to trust Jesus Christ alone for everything in life and for eternity. She just felt that Jesus could add significantly to what her other Hindu gods meant to her. Jesus could give her eternal salvation, the Holy Spirit could help her live a holier life and keep her safe from evil spirits, but Ram, Shiva, Ganesh and others also had areas of life where they could help.

In our modern globalized world, even a very English church may find itself attracting someone from another faith. Life in Britain is so multi-ethnic and multi-religious. When we go to a doctor's surgery or to a hospital, it is very possible that we shall be seen by someone from an ethnic minority. At work, or in our university or college, we may well find ourselves working together with a Hindu, Buddhist, Muslim or Jew.

Of course many of us have had to learn a little about other religions at school. Sadly, however, most of our religious teachers have little or no personal experience of living and working in a Buddhist or Muslim society. Their teaching normally comes straight from some book or course outline which gives the basic teachings of each religion, but does not relate to the grass-roots thoughts and feelings of that religion's followers. In practice most people's faith has grown out from traditional stories which they started to hear and learn when they were still children.

Jewish and Christian children are reared on the exciting stories of the Bible – creation, the fall, Noah's ark, Abraham's call to sacrifice Isaac, and so many others through the Old and New Testaments. Sabbath and Sunday schools, as well as bedtime stories, enthral our children with these wonderful accounts of the lives of our biblical heroes. What a delight it is to sit on the sofa with a child or two cuddled up next to us, perhaps with a children's Bible! The child or children will be enthralled as we recount one of the exciting Bible stories to them, and that story will never be forgotten! Through such gripping narratives children grow in their appreciation of the realities of their faith. They will not normally be taught much in the way of doctrinal truth or theology, but they will learn to know God in their own child-like way, and will grow in their appreciation of what God wants and does not want in our lives. So the biblical stories learned as a child become the foundation for a person's faith even after he or she has become an adult. In narrating Bible stories parents, 'aunties' and Christian leaders need to learn to make them come alive and also relate to the issues of our day.

Of course stories are not the only influence on a child's growth in the faith. The outward forms and rituals of the synagogue and church, the Holy Days of Judaism or Christianity (e.g. Sabbath, Passover and the other festivals for Jews, and Christmas and Easter particularly for Christians), add further colour to a child's faith. The lived-out example in the lives of parents, friends and family plays the most significant role in shaping our children's feelings and understanding in relation to their spiritual life.

Judaism finds the main source of its stories in the Old Testament, while Christians find their gold in both the Old and New Testaments. In the globalized world of the twenty-first century we enjoy the challenge and friendship of people of many different faiths. No longer can our studies be restricted to the twin biblical faiths of Judaism and Christianity. We live today in societies with multitudes of people from all over the world. Muslim mosques, Hindu and Buddhist temples, and Sikh gurdwaras vie for space in our cities together with our traditional churches and synagogues. Other faiths now form a significant part of our religious scene. As Christians, therefore, we have to relate what we believe to a great variety of other truth claims.

Our nine-year-old granddaughter's school report declared that 'much of our RE has been learning about Hinduism . . . she has responded appropriately to Hindu stories and has been able to draw comparisons between the Hindu and Christian faiths'. In the context of the study of Hinduism, her report said that she was seeking to interpret the biblical parables of Jesus. We noted how she was not being taught the parables in their own right, but in relation to her study of Hindu stories. Likewise her twelve-year-old sister's school report stressed how they were 'exploring Abrahamic faiths' and studying Buddhism. With considerable humour she told us how the whole class had been instructed in how to meditate in Buddhist fashion with the aim of achieving the peace of total non-feeling, emotionless emptiness. With their strong Christian home and church background, our grandchildren were seeking to maintain their biblical faith in Jesus, but as adult Christians we should be helping our young people in this very multi-faith school context. And what will non-Christians carry into life from their teaching at school? This background must influence the content of our evangelistic witness if we really want to scratch where people today are itching. Our gospel needs indeed to be 'good news' for contemporary society. Our witness must answer not just our traditional questions, but also those questions which stand out in our globalized, multi-faith world.

After a sermon in our village church helping Christians to understand Eastern religions' teaching on karma and reincarnation, a teenage girl in the congregation commented that 'everyone in my class at school believes in karma and reincarnation'. The sermon had started with the story of my wife's great-aunt practising the piano as a small girl in India. A large cobra was attracted by the music and was sliding towards her. Her father instructed their gardener to kill the snake, but the man did nothing. After the girl's father had killed the snake, he asked the gardener why he had not wanted to help. 'How do I know?' he replied. 'Perhaps my grandmother was reincarnate as that snake.' His belief in reincarnation could have cost the little girl her life.

Inevitably the beliefs of other religions seep into the atmosphere of our country. Buddhist and Hindu ideas of reincarnation and karma have become common in the thinking of ordinary Western people. Yoga and non-Christian meditation are offered by the National Health Service and influence many people. While Buddhism and Hinduism quietly infiltrate the ordinary everyday thought-patterns of our people, Muslims often challenge us in a more direct manner. Their community leaders do not hesitate to claim their rights according to our laws of free speech and religious freedom. In their sometimes aggressive witness they directly deny the Christian belief in the Trinity, the divinity of Jesus Christ and the reliable authority of the Bible as God's Word. In this way we may be compelled to defend our Christian faith in the context of Muslim attacks. We shall have to explain for our Muslim friends what we really believe about the Trinity, Jesus as the Son of God, and God's revelation in the Bible. If Christians do not understand other faiths and are unable to relate their own Christian faith to that context, they may find it hard to witness or even to stand firmly as believers in Jesus Christ.

To do all this, we cannot afford to remain ignorant of other religions. It has become vitally important for us as Christians to understand their often quite different beliefs, practices and worldviews. We shall therefore find it helpful to know the stories which have formed their thinking. And in our multi-ethnic situation today we shall meet people of other faiths. If we are to witness relevantly, we need to understand what other faiths believe, for otherwise our witness will scratch where they do not itch. Our gospel will be irrelevant to their felt needs. We shall be answering questions which they are not asking.

In this chapter we shall look particularly at the main faiths which we as Christians may encounter in our schools, universities and workplaces. It is also very possible that our neighbours in the flat upstairs or the house next door may belong to an ethnic minority with another religious faith. We shall see that the followers of other faiths also learn their religion through their foundational stories, together with the worship practices they observe. Likewise their young people will be deeply influenced by what they may see in the lives and relationships of their family and co-religionists. We can only relate to them and share the truth of Jesus with them if we understand them and their background.

Hinduism

'That's ridiculous. Nobody could think that way,' the students laughed as I taught about Hinduism. Afterwards one of the English students came in tears to me, sobbing, 'How could they laugh? Although I have been a Christian for years, I think like that.' Her great-grandparents came from a Hindu family background and her church's teaching had never related to her underlying Hindu thought-forms which she herself had imbibed as a child. 'I find it hard to believe that the resurrection of Jesus actually happened historically. To me it feels more like an idea than a historical event,' she explained. I went through with her again what I had taught about Hinduism's disinterest in facts, being more concerned with the underlying idea behind a certain belief. For example, Hindus do not know or care whether Krishna actually lived on earth or whether he is just part of a highly significant story. As a result of liberal thought which has been subtly influenced by Eastern religions, some Western church leaders also deny the historicity of the resurrection of Jesus, considering it just a story to illustrate the concept of a God-given new life. Together we looked at how her love for Jesus and his gospel should interact with her Hindu-background worldview and philosophy. As a result her faith grew by leaps and bounds.

As increasing numbers of ethnic British people intermarry with adherents of other faiths, the influence of other religions will inevitably grow. Even after three generations my student's religious thinking still followed that of her great-grandparents. Her family had been committed Christians ever since her grandparents converted, but their Christian teaching had never come to terms with the Hindu background in the family.

It is always an almost impossible task to describe anything related to Hinduism because it takes on such an immense variety of religious and philosophical forms. But if we want to relate effectively to our Hindu neighbours, we have to make the effort to understand them. Prof. Radhakrishnan, the great Indian philosopher and ex-president of India, stresses in his writings that Hinduism can embrace monotheism, polytheism, atheism, exclusivism and pluralism, pantheism and panentheism. Today in Britain people do not seem to mind holding firmly to various different ideas, for they no longer believe in one absolute truth. Thus they may have a vague concept of heaven at the same time as believing in reincarnation. But ultimately this enormous tolerance for a wide variety of apparently mutually contradictory beliefs is usually formulated through a parabolic story. It is such stories which lie behind the beliefs of our Hindu friends.

It is commonly said that Hinduism may best be understood by the picture of various blind men seeking to describe an elephant. One man feels its tusks and says that an elephant is long in shape, hard and shiny. Another blind man feels the elephant's tail and declares that an elephant is indeed quite long, but rough in skin and flexible. Another man feels the ears and assures his hearers that an elephant is wide, flat and apt to flap about. Another feels the elephant's side and declares that an elephant is like a strong wall. None of them conveys a full picture of the reality of an elephant, but all have experienced some part of the whole. All therefore speak truth, but no-one has the whole truth. How very postmodern that Hindu concept sounds in our pluralist society! 'All religions contain truth,' people affirm, 'but none of them can claim to be the one absolute truth.' So the uniqueness of Christ comes under threat through a Hindu-influenced pluralism. As we have seen, a Hindu may therefore gladly accept Jesus and his salvation while still worshipping other gods. So we shall need in our evangelism with Hindus to show why it is right to follow Jesus alone. He not only brings salvation from sin, but also meets our needs in every area of life. We are not intolerant when we insist on Hindu converts cutting off every link with their traditional Hindu gods, for Jesus supersedes them all.

Hinduism is sometimes said to contain two fundamental streams. The deepest consists of the *Advaita* school which denies all dualism. Ultimately all Hindus must strive to attain this reality. Following the teaching and practice of the Kerala philosopher Sankara, this highest form of Hinduism believes that everything and everybody is actually Brahman, the ultimate and only existence. Nothing has separate being, for all is Brahman.

The second stream of Hinduism is lower on the ladder which may lead up to Nirvana, the almost unattainable goal in which only Brahman exists. This lower form of Hinduism is known as the *Bhakti* (devotion) school. Its adherents gain merit through acts of sacrificial love and worship for the gods. It is through this stream of Hinduism that the multitude of temples has sprung up with all their many deities and idols. In practice, virtually no Hindu ever moves beyond this outward form of their religion. Almost certainly, therefore, our Hindu friends will follow this movement in Hinduism. It is to this stream of Hinduism that our gospel must relate particularly.

But the fundamental teaching of these schools comes across not only through philosophical definitions of the nature of existence, but particularly through stories. So it is said that we are just drops of water falling into a great ocean. As we merge into the ocean we lose our separate self-identity. The drops of water cannot be distinguished in themselves. Their goal is just to become part of the ocean. The drops of water no longer exist – there is only the ocean. In our witness we shall need to show the reality of God's creation of human beings in his likeness and image. Being like him who *is*, we also *are*. And we shall continue to exist just as the ascended Jesus still remains himself in glory. We shall be changed into spiritual beings, but it will still be 'us' with Jesus eternally.

Perhaps the key story lying behind the truths of Advaita (non-dualism) and of Bhakti (devotion) concerns the various understandings of ultimate reality. In this story a man coming home in the semi-darkness of the evening thought he saw a coiled snake by his front door. Hastily he ran to find a spade with which he could kill it. But when he thrust his spade against the 'snake', he found that in fact it was only a coil of rope.

Through this story the Hindu teaching on the different levels of reality comes across. We may note three such levels.

Firstly, there is the reality of the snake in the mind of that man. He was convinced that what he saw was a snake, and this determined his actions in fetching a spade and attacking the supposed snake. Perhaps these actions may have influenced his family. Did his wife and children see the whole event and admire his courage or did they feel he was being aggressive towards a created being? To him, and perhaps also his family, the 'snake' had a level of reality, although in fact it was ultimately *maya* (an illusion). All people at times are living with such 'snakes', confident in the reality of what is actually illusory. As biblical Christians, however, we want to underline Jesus' historical reality and the fact of his incarnation, death and resurrection. Our stories are based on solid fact.

Secondly, there is the actual rope. While it remains true that we all sometimes live in the illusory unreality of the apparent snake, most of the time we live at the level of reality which is found in the coil of rope. Ultimately, however, in Hindu philosophy neither the snake nor the rope represents true reality. Neither really exists. So our witness must include our hope of life and salvation in Jesus now and for all eternity. As Christians we live in the realm of reality. God *is*, we *are*, the world around us *is*, and our eagerly awaited future *will be*.

Hinduism, however, believes that the formulaic statement that 'all is Brahman' describes the final truth and reality. So both the snake and the rope are ultimately illusory. Only Brahman has actual existence. Hindus believe that only the enlightened will break through into this truth. Only they can penetrate to the final reality that nothing, nobody really exists. Brahman alone *is*. But our God's unique existence is evidenced by the story of his activity in and for the world and his people. The overall biblical story demonstrates the truth of God who alone reigns throughout history.

The greatest influence on the lives of the Indian multitudes within the orbit of Hinduism comes from the great epic tales of the Ramayana and the Mahabharata which include the famous Bhagavad Gita. These texts thrill their hearers and readers with their vivid stories of the gods coming down to earth and their battles and experiences here on earth. They differ radically from the much more austere Upanishads with their theoretical teaching on the *advaitin* (non-dualistic) belief that all is Brahman.

As young people, most Hindus will be regaled with these exciting stories which illustrate the battle between good and evil. Hindus' actual beliefs and religious practices will normally be formed more by these epic tales than by the high-flown philosophical teachings of the Advaita school.

What Indian Hindu child has not thrilled to the exciting and romantic stories of the Ramayana with all its amazing and unexpected twists and turns! Rama's quest for the beautiful Sita teaches in its story many facets of traditional Hindu belief, but these are portrayed through the actual story rather than by verbal application. Within the main story, we are presented with various other characters which have become a vital part of Hinduism. The god Siva enters into the tale, as does the monkey god Hanuman with his monkey army. The demon giant and the Rakshasas portray the danger of demonic powers. The golden deer illustrates Shakespeare's words that 'all that glitters is not gold' – or rather that even gold may hide demonic danger.

Hidden in the folds of this wonderfully exciting story lies a great wealth of Hindu beliefs, but they penetrate into people's hearts and minds through the story rather than by

philosophical or theological treatises. This is very postmodern!
Existentialism and so postmodernism were deeply influenced
by Eastern religions. We remember how The Beatles followed
the guru trail. So we are not surprised that postmodern Europe
as well as Indian Hinduism is influenced through this kind of
romantic myth. Still today, such stories influence the religious
thinking of many in our society. We need constantly to bear
this in mind when we relate both to Hindus and to Hindu-
influenced Westerners. And our evangelistic witness needs also
to answer the questions behind these Hindu beliefs.

The other main Hindu epic is the Mahabharata which
features the ten *avatara* (incarnations) of Vishnu, the preserver
or sustainer of life. In Hindu thought there is a multitude of
such incarnations, but the ten main ones form the background
of people's religious thought and worship. When we say that
Jesus is 'God incarnate', we need to explain this carefully.
Otherwise, Hindus may think in terms of Jesus as just another
avatar (incarnation) of Vishnu. The principal avatara are: the
black and beautiful Krishna, Rama, a fish, a tortoise, a boar, a
half-man half-lion, a dwarf, an axe-wielding sage, Gautama
the Buddha, and Kalki who will come again at the end of this
aeon. The figure of Krishna has captured the hearts not only
of Hindus, but also of many Western young people who are
devoted to him and to the Indian gurus who worship him.

Children (and adults!) respond excitedly to stories like that
of the minuscule dwarf. He tricked the demon king who ruled
as an evil despot over the whole universe. 'Let me reign over
the territory which I can cover in three strides,' pleaded the
dwarf. The demon king smiled as he looked at the dwarf's
tiny legs. Surely he would not be able to reach beyond just
a few yards! When the dwarf gained this concession, he
miraculously extended his legs and with three giant strides
circled the whole earth, thus liberating the world from the

clutches of the demons. Of course it is not difficult to formulate a theology from this delightful tale, but in practice it is the story itself which speaks. No application is needed. In this way the beliefs of Hinduism mould the lives of Hindus and many Westerners. As Christians, however, we believe that it is Jesus by his Spirit who can deliver the world from the power of evil and demonic spirits. Many of us delight to tell the Christmas story of Jesus as God's incarnate Son, but fail to mention how he saves us from the binding oppression of evil spirits. The Gospel stories of Jesus casting out evil spirits are highly relevant for Hindus, as indeed for many people of every background.

In Western forms of Hinduism it is Krishna's stories which rise above all the others. In India, Krishna is just one of the avatara and takes his place in the panoply of the gods. But he gains considerable popularity in India too because he features as the key figure in the highly popular Bhagavad Gita scriptures.

The stories of the avatara are told and retold to multitudes of Indian children, so their minds are formed through these well-known fables. People may be aware that deeper philosophical concepts lie behind the stories and undergird the faith of the *pandits*, the top philosophical leaders of Hinduism. But most people never penetrate beyond the stories. It is these fascinating stories which form the basis for temple worship and popular religion. No great intellectual prowess is needed to assimilate such epic teaching, although profound philosophy can also be attached to the child-friendly narratives.

It is, then, through these stories that popular Hinduism is understood. They are also influencing European religious thought quite significantly. They have even featured in a long series on British television. As Christians, we need to relate our witness and biblical teaching to them.

Buddhism

'What is that?' the Buddha asked Ananda, his favourite disciple. Pointing out the apparently obvious, Ananda replied, 'It is a chariot, Master.'

'Ananda, what are those?' the Buddha continued as he pointed towards the wheels. 'They are wheels, Master,' came the reply. 'Remove them!' ordered the Buddha.

'What is that?' came the next question from the Buddha.

'It is the axle, Master.'

'Remove it!' ordered the Buddha.

'What are those?' elicited the response, 'The shafts, Master' and then the command, 'Remove them!'

Finally all the constituent parts of the chariot had been identified and removed. Then came the climactic question: 'Ananda, where is the chariot?'

With deep significance Ananda replied, 'There is no chariot, Master.'

This incident teaches the central Buddhist belief of *anatta* (non-being) without any need for further preaching, teaching or explanatory application. Nothing has any existence in itself. Everything and everybody consist merely in their several constituent parts. But then each part also has no self-existence, but merely contains its various parts. And then in their turn . . . Finally we come to the ultimate Buddhist assertion of *anatta* – nothing is. Hinduism maintained that nothing has any separate self-existence, but rather that 'all is Brahman'. Buddhism goes one step further and says that the only ultimate reality is that nothing exists at all. Not even Brahman exists. The ultimate is *Sunyata* (the Void) – total emptiness and nothingness. 'There is no chariot, Master.'

Unfortunately our churches and Christian fellowships rarely tackle issues related to Buddhism, although it attracts quite large numbers of Western people. It is commonly asserted that many more British people convert to Buddhism than to Islam or any other faith. In Europe, a Sunday school programme is also very unlikely to relate the biblical stories to the questions which Buddhism or other religions present to our children. In our witness and teaching these days emphasis needs to be given to the strong biblical teaching on the nature of God as YHWH/Jehovah who reveals himself as 'I am that I am'. He has full reality with perfect existence. And he creates us in his image. We exist, and our future hope is that we shall enjoy perfect God-like existence, eternal life. Our goal is not to escape from reality and existence, as in Buddhism.

The graphic pictorial teaching of Buddhism has been encapsulated in the well-known image of the lotus flower. The beauty of the lotus delights the eye. It seems hardly credible that such delicate beauty could rise out of a sea of filthy mud. But it is true that lotus flowers generally flourish in muddy swamps. Any possibility of enlightenment emerges, Buddhists believe, from the mire of continual suffering. As with the chariot, so too the picture of the lotus flower conveys its teaching without the need for any further philosophical explanation.

Siddhartha Gautama, the Buddha, was born and brought up in the extreme luxury of a royal palace in India. But he became aware of the desperate corruption which pervaded the life of the royal court with its sensuous entertainments and personal indulgence. One day he rode his horse out into the surrounding country and was horrified there to see a destitute beggar, another man who was desperately sick, a corpse and the wasting figure of an extreme ascetic. From these shattering experiences the Buddha came to formulate his fundamental belief that 'All is *dukkha* (suffering)'. Suffering lies at the heart of all life. Suffering, Buddhism maintains, results from *tanha* (desire or thirst) – desire for food, sex, comfort and so on. Tanha drives us into continual existence and being. This existence carries on, with suffering, from one life to another into the future, in the prison of *samsara* (reincarnation). And so we are locked into the relentless cycle of rebirth. The story of the Buddha's encounters on that day has shaped people's beliefs through to our day.

It is in this context that we have to take care how we explain the Christian belief that those who put their faith in Jesus the Messiah will surely have eternal life. To the Hindu or Buddhist this sounds more like a threat than a promise! Facing the near-eternal suffering of the chain of one incarnation after another, the thought of eternal life sounds ominous indeed. We are challenged with the question of how we can present the gospel of salvation in a Buddhist-influenced society. The reality of God's creation of the world often starts a Buddhist's search for God. Creation shows that there is a beginning to everything; life is not an endless circle with no beginning or end. The creation story does not stand against a proper view of evolution. Nor does it merely teach the power of God. It also gives hope of release from the never-ending 'wheel of becoming' (which we discuss below). In the grace of our loving God we know that life may contain times of suffering, but we also experience deep joys and happiness in life. And we always have the God-given hope that our times of suffering will give way to more positive times; there is always light at the end of the tunnel. The cross is followed by the resurrection and ascension, so that the ultimate climax lies in the perfect glory of God. In the presence of God there is no more *dukkha* (suffering); all tears are wiped away.

In her later years my mother suffered from acute arthritis and could only walk with pain and the aid of sticks. In many ways life was indeed filled with 'dukkha'. When she died we

were in the process of reading C. S. Lewis's *The Last Battle* in
which he describes the utter delight of climbing up the final
waterfall to the glory above. We pictured my mother dancing
with joy before the Lord, and the sting of death gave way to
laughter and rejoicing for us all. Without theoretical application C. S. Lewis in his Narnia books teaches the Christian
faith so beautifully through his stories.

Buddhism is often represented as a wheel with the Buddha
in the centre. The Buddha declared that 'All is a wheel of
becoming.' The wheel may be seen to convey three aspects
of Buddhist belief. Firstly, that nothing is permanent. Secondly,
that life is like a circle which has neither beginning nor end.
Thirdly, we face again the reality that all is inescapable *dukkha*
or suffering. In such a Buddhist context we rejoice in the God
who *is*, the One who is the same yesterday, today and for ever.
With him there is only love, peace and righteousness; but it is
true that life without God leads to eternal, unending suffering.

Just as our skin is constantly rubbing off and being replaced
by fresh tissue, so Buddhism believes that everything is constantly changing. The concept of *anicca* (non-permanence)
is described by the statement of the Buddha that 'Life is a
bridge. Build no house upon it!' Because nothing and nobody
continues from one day to another, actions or words from
yesterday have no relevance to today. You and other people
concerned have all changed and in a sense are no more. Such
teaching can have devastating consequences for relationships,
including our relationship with God himself. I have found that
counselling with ex-Buddhist and Buddhist-influenced Christians has often included the need to discern the remnants of
Buddhist philosophy in their Christian faith.

Christians from such a Buddhist background face particular
struggles. Promises of faith and obedience to God may be
made in all sincerity today, but they hold no weight for

tomorrow. Nothing of today remains tomorrow. They may find it hard to develop close relationships in the church or family because no-one continues fully from one day to another. In this context, as we have seen, God's unchanging nature as the One who remains the same yesterday, today and for ever (Hebrews 13:8) shines with particular brilliance.

Buddhist children in countries like Thailand, Burma or Sri Lanka are often brought up to know the traditional tales of the Buddha's former incarnations. These are narrated in the Jatakas, a series of 547 poems with explanatory stories. In some countries, including Thailand, these are publicly performed in dance and dramatic theatre. In Thailand too there is a much-loved old art form in which two people recite a traditional myth or tale with sing-song voices. The Jatakas are commonly recited in this way.

As Christian mission workers in South Thailand, a friend of mine and I used to recite publicly the story of Jesus and his saving gospel in this form. On one occasion we recited the good news of Jesus at a large fair. Later in the evening we heard drunken voices outside our tent. A group of Buddhist Thai teenagers were mocking us by laughingly copying our recitals. We felt sad that they made fun in this way of the message of Jesus Christ, but we rejoiced that they had learned the whole poetic recital off by heart. This epic art form sticks easily in the memory. Many people could recite our epic of the life of Jesus for themselves. Some took our story and recited it back in their home area or village, so our witness was multiplied throughout the region.

The Jatakas' delightful tales of some of the Buddha's former incarnations tell of him appearing as a king, but also as an outcast. In one incarnation he appears as a god – in Buddhism the gods form a level of incarnation which is superior to mere ordinary humans, but inferior to a monk. In one's progress

upwards towards enlightenment one may pass through the
stage of being a god en route to becoming a monk.

The Jatakas contain beautiful folk tales of the Buddha's
reincarnation as a variety of animals. Children thrill to the
stories of the monkey and the crocodile, the turtle who could
not stop talking, or the crab and the crane. Their love of the
Buddha and their whole understanding of his teaching are
formed in their childhood through the Jataka stories.

Many serious books of Buddhist theory and philosophy are
based on the teachings of the Buddha and the contents of the
Buddhist scriptures. But these are largely aimed at a Western
audience and at leading Buddhist thinkers. In a way they
parallel the major theological works of Christianity, largely
produced for an ivory-tower readership. Ordinary Buddhists
never aspire to such deep works of profound philosophical
learning. They learn from the traditional stories which have
formed their minds from childhood. The Jesuits have claimed
that if they have a child until he/she is seven, they will have
him/her for life. In the same way, Buddhist minds have been
moulded in their beliefs and the practice of their faith by these
fascinating childhood tales. Likewise the visible traditional
religious rites in the temple and home become an essential
part of their whole culture.

We need to grapple with this to understand our postmodern world. Buddhist approaches have so infiltrated into
European everyday thinking that people are often not even
aware of the original source. They just think it is 'common
sense' and assume that everyone thinks in that way. The
pluralist 'supermarket mentality' has its roots in such thinking.
Buddhism promises a deep experience of peace in our frenetic
world. Emptiness can seem very peaceful! As Christians we
are challenged to show that in Jesus Christ we can experience
an even more profound sense of true peace.

In the centre of Purley, Surrey there used to be a major intersection of five main roads. They all converged with traffic lights in the centre. One day I observed a young Buddhist devotee sitting cross-legged on the traffic lights island. Surrounded by the fumes and noise of large lorries and multitudes of cars, he was meditating. He showed no sign of being aware of anything that went on around him. He was experiencing the 'peace' of losing all feeling. He felt himself on the way to the non-existence which ushers in the final Buddhist enlightenment.

A young American delved deeply into the depths of Buddhist non-existence. In a Thai temple he disciplined himself to remove all emotions. He no longer felt hot or cold, hunger or thirst, like or dislike, comfort or discomfort. His face reminded me of pictures of Holocaust survivors in a Nazi death camp with their emaciated bodies and sunken eyes without the sparkle of true feeling.

As Christians we have a message of true inner peace with a life and joy which should radiate out into the world to transform societies and people. Jesus not only promises us an ongoing life, but also assures us that he will give us a life which is abundant (John 10:10).

Zen Buddhism

Together with Sufi Muslim mysticism and the Jewish mystical Kabbalah, Zen Buddhism appeals strongly to people who are disillusioned with traditional institutional Christian faith. More modern forms of Christian meditation can satisfy positively this spiritual need, but they can also face the danger of adopting the patterns of Zen Buddhism rather than the Christian biblical teaching about waiting on the Lord. Our contemporary hunger for spirituality has made it imperative for us to know what Zen is all about.

Some years ago I was invited to be the speaker at a Swiss student conference. 'We shall be having a time of meditation each morning,' the leaders told me. They then presented me with a sheaf of papers outlining the meditations we would have in these worship times. When I got to my bedroom and read through these papers, I was horrified to note the constant references to losing self-awareness, to the need to come out from ourselves and enjoy an emptiness of mind. I underlined them all in red, handed my papers back to the leaders, and suggested that we should have a less Zen Buddhist and more Christian approach to meditation.

To teach the difference between positive Christian meditation and the forms of meditation practised in Hinduism and Buddhism, it may be helpful to distinguish how each religion might meditate on one's finger. Believing that 'all is Brahman' and therefore that the finger does not exist in itself, Hindus meditate *through* the finger. It will be their aim to lose awareness of themselves, of the action of meditating and of the finger itself. They will desire to lose self-awareness and sink into Brahman, the only one who truly exists. Buddhists go one step further in meditation. They not only seek to lose awareness of the finger, the process of meditation and of themselves. They don't believe in the existence of Brahman either, so they don't even want to lose themselves in Brahman. They look for *Sunyata* (the Void), absolute non-existent emptiness. In contrast, Christians will meditate *on* (not through!) the finger, never losing sight of themselves or of the process of meditating. As they meditate on their finger, they will rejoice in how wonderfully the Lord has created us, how he has fitted the finger so perfectly for its functions. They may also see that gradually their finger loses its beauty and sensitivity as we get older. So our praise for the Creator is mixed with a realization of our mortality, and longing for redemption. Such meditation is much more life-affirming and positive than anything experienced by Hindus or Buddhists. We have a peace that is indeed beyond understanding.

Zen Buddhists may explain their beliefs by recounting the story of a man who came to the Buddha and asked him to teach him the way of enlightenment. The Buddha leant down and picked up an old brick. He then got out a cloth and began to polish the brick. He polished it and polished it and polished it. Finally the man smiled. That smile reflected his enlightenment and reveals the heart of Zen Buddhism.

In Zen Buddhism its adherents learn that there are no means towards the goal of enlightenment. If we get stuck on an emphasis on particular means, we shall never attain the final goal. You may polish a brick as much as you can, but bricks cannot be polished. Not even meditation can be guaranteed as the way to enlightenment. When the man became aware that the Buddha was just doing the impossible by continuing to polish the brick, he smiled the smile of enlightenment.

Christians also believe that we need to go beyond mere means in our initial salvation and in our growth as disciples of Jesus. Bible reading and prayer are not in themselves a guarantee of spiritual life and growth. But on the other hand, God uses our spiritual practices to bring us his blessings. While we are saved by God's grace alone, he uses our faith as his means.

In another revealing story a man came to the Buddha, presented him with a beautiful flower made of gold, and asked him to teach him the way of enlightenment. The Buddha took the golden flower into his hands and looked at it from every angle. He continued turning the flower round and round while observing it with rapt attention. Finally this man too smiled the smile of enlightenment.

Although in Zen Buddhism there is no necessary means of enlightenment, this second man came to understand that meditation can be a route towards enlightenment.

The fundamental belief of Zen Buddhism is sometimes described in the observation that a crane has long legs and a duck has short legs. It would be ridiculous if the crane tried to shorten its legs or if the duck sought to lengthen its legs. Both in Zen Buddhism and in Chinese Taoism we are encouraged just to accept life as it is without striving to change anything. As people cease to desire change of any sort, they may come into the experience of enlightenment.

As Christians we may remember the apparently similar teaching of Jesus that we should not be anxious about our life with its everyday issues of what we should eat or wear. We are incapable of adding a single hour to our lives or a single inch to our height (Luke 12:22–31). Whereas Jesus' teaching warns against anxious worry, the story of the crane and duck is opposing all effort and desire to change things. Such passivity will militate against any concern for social reform in opposition to oppression, inequality, ecological and environmental vandalism, the tragedies of marital breakdown, abuse and so many other evils with which we are surrounded.

In the next chapter we shall see how the Bible too conveys much of its teaching through stories. Hinduism and Buddhism are not alone in this approach.

Taoism

A high proportion of Chinese people follow the religious practice of Taoism alongside their Buddhist religion and Confucian ethics. With Chinese culture's strong emphasis on education and business, Chinese people flood into all countries around the world. Tens of thousands of Chinese scholars come every year to our universities and they are generally surprisingly open to the Christian faith. Many become Christians. Some have formed their own Chinese churches, but more and more are also joining the local church where they live. In doing so, they may unconsciously introduce the religious thought-forms from their own background.

It is sometimes asserted that the heart of Taoism may be found in one very short pithy statement: 'There was a man who dreamed that he was a butterfly.'

Many Westerners with their non-pictorial backgrounds may find it difficult to unravel the depths of religious meaning in this one simple picture. It may take them a while to realize that this one sentence is in itself adequate to convey the religious beliefs of a whole faith system. When they hear the sentence, they may continue to listen intently, hoping to hear a continuation of the story.

So what are the beliefs which lie within this statement?

Firstly, curiosity is aroused by this simple idea. It leads on to the inevitable question: might it really have been a butterfly dreaming it was a man? Or was it indeed a butterfly dreaming it was a man who was having a dream of being a butterfly? Or was there really any dream at all? Were the man, the dream and the butterfly all an illusion?

Taoism and Buddhism ask similar questions about ultimate reality. When is apparent reality just a dream? These philosophical questions have penetrated deeply into the younger generation in the West. Many years ago I was asked to speak in an evangelistic coffee group among Cambridge University students. On the table before us was a jar of marmalade. After a while one of the students, influenced by Eastern religions, interrupted the flow of conversation, picked up the marmalade jar and said somewhat dreamily, 'I find it hard to believe that this jar actually exists.' Some of the other non-Christian students agreed with him and shared his doubts concerning the existence of the jar. 'I often feel that life is just one big dream,' another student added. Buddhism and Taoism have gained a subtle influence on the everyday thinking of many students. They may not realize that their worldview is Taoist in character, but actually they are influenced by this Chinese religious philosophy. To many traditional British Christians, this 'life-is-one-big-dream' view may sound incredible and even ridiculous. But particularly in witness among university students it will be important that our Christian message should understand and relate to this feeling.

The aim of Taoism is that its adherents should sink peacefully into their surrounding nature. Thus Taoist Chinese art has no clear figures standing out against the surrounding natural phenomena. Traditional Western art portrays its subject in sharp contrast against the background. Thus a depiction of Napoleon on his horse would dominate the whole picture. Royal portraits concentrate on the particular person being painted. Definite lines separate one subject from another with a distinct, stark self-existence. This would be anathema to a Taoist. In a Taoist picture the human figures are very small and in the background. No strong delineations mark out one figure from another. Trees, mountains, a river or bridge all merge into one another. Vague forms of birds or other phenomena will likewise fit into the unclear lines of the whole painting. True Taoist beauty means an acceptance that everything and everybody shares in the very nature of the Tao, the ultimate way.

The best-known Taoist story tells of a man who is so frightened of his own shadow that he tries to run away from it. In the midday sun his shadow naturally follows him wherever he goes. He may walk slowly, and his shadow insists on walking equally slowly. He runs to escape his shadow, but it continues to run at the same speed. He races as fast as his legs will carry him, but his shadow keeps pace persistently with him. In the hard glare of the sun there seems no escape from his shadow until finally he comes to stand beneath the ample branches of a tree. As he and his shadow become a part of the tree's shade and sink into the Tao of the tree, so he loses his fear and can be free of his own shadow.

This Taoist story has its parallel in Francis Thompson's well-known poem 'The Hound of Heaven', in which a man feels himself to be pursued by God and tries desperately to run away. But we may observe a fundamental difference between the two. 'The Hound of Heaven', with its Christian background, portrays a person's attempt to run away from God, not from the shadow of his own being. Many British people today are indeed frightened of any encounter with God. They feel that God might interfere with their desires for pleasure in life and restrict them to a boring and unintelligent legalism. After a long chase, finally 'The Hound of Heaven' shows how God catches up with the person, and the beauty of God's grace and goodness enters into his life. The under-lying philosophies or theologies differ fundamentally from each other. In the more Christian 'Hound of Heaven' the shadow gives way to the beautiful grace and loving kindness of the Lord. God finally gives us his perfect peace, which allows active involvement in the world, not a passive avoidance of all action. In the Taoist story the person is right to run away from his shadow and the reality of his own being, for in Taoism peace and harmony can only be found as we merge our separate self-existence into the shade of the great Tao (Way). In Francis Thompson's poem, on the other hand, it is unwise to run away from God who lovingly follows after us with his offer of life and salvation. What peace he gives us when finally we allow him to meet with us!

In the Taoist story, freedom and enlightenment come from identification with the way of the Tao. No striving to free oneself from one's own desires and enslaving self-existence can bring that liberty which can only come from a total oneness with the Tao. Again we notice that this religious philosophy is largely portrayed through stories and paintings. In our society, which is frenetic, over-busy and stressed, it is no wonder that such Eastern religions appeal so strongly to postmodern Westerners. A longing for peace underlies contemporary Western life. As Christians we are called to demonstrate the peace of God in our daily living, so that others may see true peace in practice even in the midst of busy lives. It may prove helpful to recount the story of 'The Hound of Heaven' in conversation with our neighbours, making it clear in the story that it is God who wants to catch up with us and give us his peace.

As Christians we can be like a submerged submarine beneath a stormy sea. The wind above can howl and the waves can crash into the depths, but the submarine moves forward in peace beneath it all.

Islam

In Europe today Islam commonly claims our attention. Its leaders boldly demand special treatment in the provision of *halal* food, special prayer rooms and the right for Muslim women to wear particular clothing. On a university campus it is very possible that Muslim students will seek to convert you to Islam. Islamic terrorism and violence are never far from our minds as we follow world news. Militant Muslims also push their faith in our prisons. As Christians in the modern world we have to face the challenge of Islam and learn how to answer Muslim attacks against our belief in the Trinitarian God and in our Bible.[3]

More and more people in Africa and some countries of Europe are becoming Muslim. This challenges Christians to show why the Christian faith outshines Islam. At the same time, growing numbers of Muslims are turning to Jesus Christ in North Africa, Central Asia and various other countries. In Britain, too, Iranians and other Muslims are becoming Christians and need discipling. Traffic grows in both directions on the bridge between Islam and the Christian faith. No longer is knowledge of Islam only for missionaries and other overseas workers. Ordinary British Christians and particularly students also need to learn about Islam.

From an early age most Muslim children and young people are expected to attend their local Qur'anic school. The teaching methods may hardly suit their European surroundings and may be accompanied by violence and beatings. But here the pupils receive careful instruction on the Qur'an and how to recite it in its original Arabic language. They learn much of the Qur'an off by heart, and many children will even succeed in being able to recite the whole book. This is no mean feat even for students who have Arabic as their mother tongue. But the majority of Muslims in Britain and elsewhere in the world do not speak Arabic at home. For them it is a foreign language, so it is by no means easy to learn to recite the words accurately, with the right intonation and pronunciation. Any small error even in such linguistic details will mean that they forfeit the blessing which Muslims believe they will gain from reciting the Holy Book. Indeed, any such errors may be considered blasphemy as the Qur'an is believed to be the exact writing of Allah himself. And blasphemy is a major sin, with serious consequences.

Although students who do not speak Arabic at home with their families may successfully learn to recite the Qur'an correctly in the original language, they may never understand what they have learned off by heart.

My wife and I were kindly invited to visit a small fishing village in the most strictly Muslim part of Malaysia. Our Malay friends fetched us in their fishing boats and then took us to the village coffee shop. Here we were quickly surrounded by a dozen or more local fishermen who were curious to meet us and talk with us.[4] After a while the headman began to tell us with considerable pride about his oldest son. He called his wife and asked her to fetch this son so that we might admire him too. So we were presented with a somewhat shy young lad aged about twelve. The headman told us how this boy had learned the whole Qur'an off by heart and could recite it with absolute perfection.

It was clearly the time for me to play the part of an electioneering politician. Having often seen such individuals showing their interest in the local children, I too patted the boy on the shoulder and congratulated him on his achievement. I had no hesitation in sharing the headman's admiration for the boy's ability in learning the whole book in Arabic, when he had no knowledge at all of that language.

'Does he understand what he has learned by heart?' I ventured to ask the headman after I had properly shown my admiration for his son. What a strange and unexpected question! The little knot of men looked up with eager interest from their glasses of coffee. Why is this foreigner asking such a stupid question? Of course the boy cannot possibly understand the language of the Qur'an! And does it matter? Surely he will gain the *baraka* (blessing) of God just by reciting the words of Allah in the Qur'an. You don't need to understand it, for these are the very words which Allah revealed to his prophet Mohammed. To share with God in reciting exactly the divine words of God himself must bring the fullness of God's blessing and power.

I could just feel the minds of those men reacting with religious assurance to my question – and yet I felt their curiosity growing. Was I somehow coming at the question of rote learning of the Qur'an from an angle that was different from their traditional approach?

I followed up my question with another one: 'Does God want to teach us his ways through the Qur'an? Does Allah desire to communicate with us? Or is he so *akbar* [great] that he doesn't build any relationship with us as mere weak human beings?' Muslims believe that we are made of clay and are therefore insignificantly small. What communication can there be between an elephant and an ant?

Such questions led naturally to the Christian belief that God does indeed want to speak to us. He longs to make himself known to us in order that we might be reconciled to him and form a living relationship with him. When we returned to the mainland we were able to send the headman a New Testament in the Malay language.

If the local Qur'anic school is only teaching children to recite the Qur'an in Arabic without helping them to understand its teaching, where do such ordinary Muslim children gain their religious understanding in countries which do not speak Arabic?

Muslim children's understanding of their faith is actually being formed through traditional stories. All over the Muslim world the stories of the life of Mohammed grip the minds and hearts of children and young people. These are found in two sources – the Sirat Mohammed (the story of his life) and the Hadith (the traditions of the thoughts, words and deeds of Mohammed) – both of which date from around the same time.

After the death of Mohammed, which ended the Qur'anic revelations, it was found that the Qur'an did not have adequate answers to all the questions and disputes in the community. It was felt that the life of the prophet, God's ideal messenger, would provide the needed guidance. So the Muslims gathered from his wives and companions everything they could glean about him. These traditions were written down in four books of Hadith, the best known of which are the Sahih Al-Bukhari and the Sahih Muslim. Together with the Qur'an itself, the Hadith forms the authoritative revelation of God. Its stories determine the whole life and practice of Muslims all over the world.

Also, about a hundred years after the death of Mohammed in AD 632 the *sirat* (life story) of Mohammed was written down by various authors, the most popular and influential of which was Ibn-Ishaq. He was born in Medina, and lived in Alexandria and also in Baghdad where he died in the 760s. While the Gospels recounted the life and teaching of Jesus within a generation after his death, Ibn-Ishaq only wrote down the story of Mohammed's life more than a century later.

In this authoritative but somewhat hagiographical story of the life of Mohammed, Ibn-Ishaq works his way through from the early life of Mohammed in Mecca and his marriage to the rich widow Khadijah to his hearing of the Qur'anic revelations and the *Hijra* (the migration from Mecca to Medina). Considerable space is given over too to the key battles which Mohammed fought against the people of Mecca before he finally gained the victory, marched triumphantly into Mecca and performed both the Little and the Great *Hajj* (pilgrimage). The story ends with Mohammed's final illness and death. This contrasts markedly with the Gospels, in which the death of Jesus is not the conclusion. For Jesus and his followers, death gives way to the glory of the resurrection.

The stories of the Sirat have chapters devoted to key topics of Islamic teaching. They cover the issue of waging war and the major matter of *jihad* (struggle), and also questions of prayer, *zakat* (alms giving), the *Hajj* (pilgrimage), opposition to the Trinity and therefore the Muslim emphasis on *tawhid* (the indivisible oneness of Allah which is the central tenet of Islam). The Sirat also has a major chapter on revelation. Muslims believe God revealed his will in the four major books of the Taurat (the Law) through the prophet Musa (Moses); then came the Zabur (Psalms) through the prophet Da'ud (David); these led on to the Injil (Gospel) through the prophet Isa (Jesus); and finally the greatest and climactic revelation in the Qur'an through the seal of the prophets, Mohammed himself.

Christians will notice that the books' names clearly relate to the biblical Torah (Law), Mizmor (Psalms) and Euaggelion (Gospel). Muslims believe that, because of the disobedience and sin of God's people, each of these books became inoperative and therefore God revealed a new book (the Qur'an) to replace it. Unfortunately we have to confess that such replacement theology has also gained considerable ground in Christian circles. Many Christians believe that the New Testament has replaced the Old Testament because of the sin of Israel in rejecting Jesus as Messiah. So the new covenant in the blood of Christ would replace the old covenant with Israel. The logical conclusion of such mistaken theology would be that the new covenant in Jesus would also need replacing, because of the whole history of sin in the church! No, as Christians we believe in the whole Bible as the unchanging Word of God still today.

It is noteworthy too that in Islam revelation is believed to be *through* the prophets, not *by* the author of a book. In Muslim belief the Qur'an was written by God in heaven before the

creation. Indeed the Qur'an is said to be God's eternal and
uncreated perfect word. Mohammed was merely the channel
through whom God sent down his revelation. The Qur'an has
no human input. That is why it is thought to be so very holy.
Merely reciting it therefore brings enormous *baraka* (blessing).

Together with the narrative teaching of the Hadith and
the Sirat, from the outset of the history of Islam there have
been major theological and philosophical writings which
teach the Muslim faith in more conceptual terms. Some even
used the patterns of Greek philosophy to express their faith.
Thus the great Al-Ghazali (1058–1111) used Aristotelian
dialectics to express his theological treatises, as did the Christian theologian Thomas Aquinas (1225–74) and the leading
Jewish theologian Moses Maimonides, the Rambam (1135–
1204). But it has to be said that multitudes of Muslims
around the world gain their understanding of Islam's theological beliefs more through the practice of the mosque
and the stories of the life of Mohammed in the Hadith and
the Sirat.

Just as most Muslims have learned their faith through the
stories of Mohammed, so also in our witness with our Muslim
neighbours we need to win them with the biblical stories of
Jesus. Nothing in Islam can compare with the down-to-earth
reality and heavenly glory of the stories of Jesus' life, miracles,
relationships and teachings. And when our Muslim friends
have seen the beauty of the human Jesus, then we can move
on to his incarnation, the glory of his sacrificial death for us,
his life-giving resurrection and our ascension with him into
the very presence of the Father. Our stories of the powerful
working of his Holy Spirit in our lives and the lives of other
Christians will put the icing on the gospel cake.

The first beginnings of the church in Java, Indonesia may
illustrate the powerful potential of the stories of Jesus in the

Gospels. Now these churches run into the millions of members, all of whom come from a Muslim background. But when Gottlob Bruckner (1783–1857) worked in Java, there were no local Christians. Settling on the north coast of the island in Semarang, he struggled to learn the extremely complex Javanese language and then translated the New Testament into Javanese. He then had some of the stories of the life of Jesus printed – each story was related as a small tract on its own with no explanation or application. Two of these tracts somehow fell into the hands of people in two large villages. Through reading just the one miracle of Jesus, hundreds of Muslims became followers of Jesus in each village. Of course their faith was somewhat inadequate, for it was built on just that one story and they knew nothing about the rest of the life, relationships and teaching of Jesus. But they came to love Jesus enough to leave Islam and follow him. After some years, Dutch pastors discovered these two churches and gave them more teaching.

Just telling a story of Jesus from the New Testament can play a significant part in drawing Muslims to faith in Jesus. Many Muslims suffer because of evil spirit activity, so the stories of Jesus casting out evil spirits can offer them new hope of deliverance. While it remains true that conversion to Jesus Christ will usually bring fierce persecution, the prospect of freedom from demonic oppression will be very attractive. In sharing with Muslims we always run the danger of being restricted to debate on the great theological issues of the incarnation, the Trinity and the reliability of the Bible. But Jesus' life and miracles are so glorious and are what we want to communicate to our Muslim friends. His sacrificial death and resurrection for us are wonderful and can captivate not only our hearts, but also Muslims'. Jesus is so much more wonderful than anything to be found in Islam. Let us therefore

take every possible opportunity of telling the stories of Jesus'
life, death and resurrection!

Questions:

- How could you and your church have a more effective
  witness among ethnic minority people in your area?
- Which religion(s) most influence the thinking of the
  people around you? Make a point of learning more of
  that particular faith.

4. BIBLICAL PATTERNS OF TEACHING

'Do you happen to have any Haggadah?' the potential customer asked the Jewish bookshop attendant. 'Yes, of course,' came the immediate reply, and the attendant led the customer to one particular shelf in a prominent section of the shop's display. The term Haggadah refers to books of the Passover Seder liturgy.

Sadly, for Christians the word 'liturgy' fails to thrill us with the exciting expectation of dynamic symbolic action. Yet in baptism services we enjoy the drama of watching people being immersed in water or having water sprinkled on their heads. In the Lord's Supper or Communion service we richly enjoy the symbolic representations of Jesus' body and blood in the bread and wine. And we are moved by the act of eating and drinking the bread and wine together with the whole congregation.

Doubtless all Christians hold in their memories some particular experience of the Lord's Supper which had special meaning for them. My mind goes back to a small congregation in Laos. The 'bread' took the form of irregular sticky rice balls, and the 'wine' was a very cheap and nasty orange squash served in glasses which were far from smart or hygienic. The glasses stood on a terribly tasteless round tray of vivid blue and orange colours. By the time I partook of the 'wine' the glasses had all been emptied, but the squash had been spilled liberally onto the tray. Along with others, I duly partook of the wine by tipping the tray and drinking directly from it. I rejoiced anew in the wonder of our fellowship as Christians both with one another and within the church of God. Such love together does not in any way depend on the smartness or correctness of the outward forms.

My spine still tingles at the memory of a large and fast-growing church in China. The church was growing so fast that every Sunday they welcomed many more people than had come on the previous weekend. As a result they had little idea how many people they should cater for when they celebrated the Lord's Supper. They used cream crackers as the 'bread'. By the time the plate had reached us, towards the back of the crowded church, the crackers had been broken and broken and broken . . . Only tiny crumbs remained and they were too small to pick up. We watched as the plate was passed from person to person down the line until it reached us. Each person licked the tip of a finger and in this way got hold of a tiny crumb. We in our turn did the same and so shared the body of Christ with our sisters and brothers in that congregation. What a privilege! And what a way to learn of the rapid growth of the churches in China! An objective talk on the growth of the church in China would not have impressed itself on us as strongly.

The Passover Seder too is not just a dry 'liturgy'. It is packed with deeply impressive symbolic action. In fact, it is so action-packed that even small children are fascinated by it all. There is no need to send them out to a special children's Sabbath school or Sunday school.

The children particularly enjoy searching for the carefully hidden *afikomen*, the middle of the three sections of the matzah. The child who finds it brings it back in triumph to his or her father and bargains with him for its return. A child also asks the traditional questions about why we celebrate this day. We are reminded of the ten plagues in Egypt as we all dip our fingers into a cup of wine and release a drop onto our plate, one for each plague as it is described.

The Seder takes place in the context of a delicious meal, and a central plate has on it key elements to symbolize different experiences in Egypt. Thus bitter herbs like horse-radish bring tears to the eyes in memory of Israel's bitter slavery in Egypt; parsley or celery dipped in salt water represents the actual pain of that slavery; *charoset*, a mixture of chopped nuts, grated apple, cinnamon and red wine, reminds us of the mud with which the Israelites made bricks in their slavery; a hard-boiled egg stands for mourning in Jewish symbolism; while a shank bone brings us to the sacrificial lamb associated with Passover.

Such very visible elements not only entertain and keep children's (and adults'!) attention. They make the teaching of God's deliverance from slavery memorable. It could be claimed that this teaching of the exodus and God's salvation from all forms of slavery form the heart of the Jewish faith – and are a foretaste of the gospel. The Christian message too needs to be communicated not only through words, but also through visible signs and drama.

But Haggadah is actually more than just the Passover Seder.

Haggadah

In our understanding of the Bible and in our witness to biblical truth we need to have a good grasp of the Bible ourselves. Of course the foundation for this begins with an understanding of the purpose of the original writers in their particular context. Only when we have seen what the Bible meant to its writers and their audiences can we proceed to unpack what the text means for us today.

'We Jews wrote the Scriptures, so it can't be entirely wrong to look at the Bible through Jewish eyes,' declared the speaker with an encouraging smile as he recommended a Jewish book on one of the Gospels.

The original writers, and those who received their writings, were indeed Jews, so it may prove helpful for us to get to grips with traditional Jewish ways of teaching.

The Passover Seder is the supreme example of Haggadah, but haggadic teaching is really much wider. It includes all teaching by means of stories, dramatic actions, pictorial representations and parabolic teaching. Haggadic stories may be true historical events or they may be more like parables or illustrations of truth. It stands, therefore, in contrast to Halachah. Halachic teaching is through direct legal injunctions – do this! Don't do that! – and non-pictorial concepts or facts.

The Bible is of course written by Jews, and therefore these basic teaching approaches lie behind the contents both of the Old Testament and the New Testament. As we shall see, biblical truth is conveyed throughout Scripture both by the more popular haggadic forms and by halachic teaching. In preaching, teaching or any other form of Christian witness it is imperative that our words bring people the full truth of God's revealed good news. But it is also important that our witness reflects biblical patterns of communication. There is a danger that our biblical exposition and particularly our theological thought can fail to mirror the Bible's emphasis on Haggadah. Western Christians may even be tempted to feel that haggadic communication is only for children and cannot be used for more intellectually challenging teaching. In telling stories we may give an impression of not conveying intelligent truth. Biblical stories, however, have stood the test of centuries, and even brilliant theologians still struggle to understand the full significance of many of the biblical narratives.

'Traditional evangelical teaching has in the past declared that we should go to the Epistles as the basis for good theological teaching,' I declared in a lecture. 'Then we look at the Gospels and the Acts of the Apostles for the historical background to that teaching. But in more recent times we have all come to understand that the Gospels and Acts also have theological axes to grind. If our biblical scholars and those who teach and preach the Christian faith had only known their Jewish didactic theory, they would never have said such things,' I continued rather strongly.

'But you wrote in your earlier book, *Don't Just Stand There*, exactly what you have just denied,' countered one of the students. 'You wrote that the Epistles reveal theology, while the Gospels provide the historical background.' He then quoted what I had written, giving the page and line reference in the book.

With some embarrassment I had to admit that in the past I had not queried the teaching of my theological lecturers or of the preachers I heard in those early days. That is the danger of writing books! What one thinks at the time of writing is set down in black and white. But hopefully one's thinking grows as the years slip by. We can still realize how wrong we have been, and develop our understanding of the biblical faith.

So I have had to repent of my former error, and that I have taught my students what is clearly untrue. Biblical teaching comes to us both in haggadic and halachic forms. Every part of the Bible reveals God's truth, and in communicating our Christian faith we need to follow biblical patterns.

As we have already noted, the Bible starts with major haggadic teaching in the account of God's creation of the world. This is not just given so that we might know how the universe started. The account contains much teaching about God and humanity, the relationship between men and women, environmental and ecological responsibility, the knowledge of good and evil, the fall and sin. None of these great theological matters is developed in halachic form, for haggadic teaching can be sufficient in itself.

The same could be said of the whole Old Testament account of the history of God's people from the early Genesis accounts of prehistory through to the exile to Babylon. These stories are not there just to satisfy historical curiosity, but to teach God's people the whole gamut of God's truth.

So, in the exodus and during Israel's forty years of wandering in the wilderness, God places himself in the midst of his people or goes before them in a cloud of fire. The Old Testament carefully records how the cloud dwells in the midst of Israel when they are encamped, but goes in front of them when they are to strike camp and proceed to their next location. The narrative describes God's ordering how the tribes are to encamp around the cloud. Each tribe is to have its particular station in relation to the cloud of God. Nowhere does the Old Testament actually say that this relates to the cultural patterns of the various other peoples of that area of the world at that time. Yet among those other nations the king would normally march in front of his whole people during the day, but at night with all the dangers of darkness his people would be carefully ordered to camp around him to protect him from attack. With the other nations too, each tribe or family would be allocated a special position in the protective circles around the king. In following this cultural pattern of the surrounding nations, God was making it clear to his people that he was their King. They needed no other human king, for God himself filled that supreme position in their national life. This important teaching, which foreshadows the whole theology of the kingdom of God, is taught not only by abstract halachic theology, but rather by the more visual haggadic approach.

In the Bible, haggadic and halachic forms of teaching are interlaced. Both are important in communicating the truth. Thus the Old Testament historical books not only convey God's truth through the historical stories of God's dealings with Israel, but also through long sections of God's detailed commandments concerning the construction of the Tent of Meeting, the offering of the various sacrifices, and legal prescriptions for the welfare of the congregation of Israel. As we shall see, this interlacing of Halachah and Haggadah carries on also into the New Testament. In a European context people are not accustomed to teaching through stories without a specific application, so it may prove particularly important to add halachic teaching to our stories or acted dramatic teaching. We have already noted C. S. Lewis's brilliant story-form teaching, but many Europeans have read the Narnia books or seen the film of *The Lion, the Witch and the Wardrobe* without understanding the significance of the story. Christians can helpfully use his stories, but we may need to explain their meaning.

God himself uses various visible things to bring his teaching before the people. We see this when Joshua chooses one man from each of the twelve tribes of Israel and commands him to carry a stone with him, to erect a memorial pillar to keep God's miracle-working power before the eyes of the people.

Indeed God's purpose with the stones went further than just Israel. He desired 'that all the peoples of the earth might know that the hand of the LORD is powerful' (Joshua 4:24). God's missionary purpose that all nations might 'fear the LORD your God' was already evident through the visible sign of those stones. It should, however, also be noted that the visible sign (Haggadah) is further taught by straight conceptual explanation (Halachah) at the end of the chapter.

The prophets

This combination of Halachah and Haggadah may be observed in the writings of the prophets. We often think that the prophetic books largely contain conceptual teaching: warnings of God's impending judgment on sinful Israel, and encouragement that the grace and merciful loving kindness of the Lord continues. Excitingly, they also prophesy the coming of the Servant Messiah. But this is often expressed in vivid pictorial language and dramatic action.

Thus Isaiah sings a song about a vineyard (Isaiah 5:1–7). This haggadic passage is then explained in halachic fashion. The vineyard, 'the garden of his delight', is shown to represent Israel. God looked to his vineyard for the fruit of justice and righteousness, but only 'saw bloodshed' and 'heard cries of distress'. Then God reveals the tragedy of his judgment being poured out on his own chosen people, the ones he delighted in. What rich teaching comes across through this simple agricultural picture!

Jeremiah and Ezekiel use dramatic action to bring God's teaching to their contemporaries. For example, Jeremiah buys a linen belt and puts it round his waist (Jeremiah 13). He is then commanded to hide it 'in a crevice in the rocks'. After a considerable time he was commanded to dig up the belt, but found it 'ruined and completely useless'. This vivid action is further applied in 13:8–11. God has bound Israel like a belt around himself, but they have worshipped other gods and become 'completely useless'. So God will bring down their pride in judgment.

Perhaps we too can use dramatic action to convey God's teaching. For many years our family used to act out the Christmas story each year. What fun we all had in this simple presentation of the Christmas story! Such acted stories could become a regular part not only of family life, but also in our churches. It doesn't need to be very professional if it is only performed within the congregation. In this way we reinforce our biblical teaching.

Isaiah and Jeremiah

Jeremiah's ministry began with God calling and teaching him in a distinctly haggadic way. He was shown an almond branch and a boiling pot. With an obvious play on the Hebrew words, the almond branch conveys the reassuring message that God's Word will be fulfilled. The boiling pot spilling its contents out from the north makes it clear that disaster will be meted out through the ravages of peoples attacking Israel from the north (Jeremiah 1:11–15).

In Jeremiah's call, God reaches out his hand, touches Jeremiah's mouth and speaks to him without an intermediary. From our reading of his prophecy, Jeremiah seems to have lacked self-assurance. So God kindly meets with him in this direct, unmediated fashion.

On the contrary, the gifted Isaiah may have been tempted to pride. So God calls him to the prophetic ministry through the shattering experience of the huge temple building shaking in an earthquake-like experience with the flashing seraphim

calling 'Holy, Holy, Holy' to each other in the smoke. No
wonder Isaiah is brought low with the deep realization that
he is 'a man of unclean lips' who is also living among a 'people
of unclean lips'. God does not deal directly with Isaiah. He
sends a seraph who, with tongs, takes a coal from the altar:
God – seraph – tongs – altar – coal – Isaiah (Isaiah 6:1–7).

God's dealings both with Isaiah and Jeremiah are distinctly
haggadic in character.

Ezekiel

When we come to Ezekiel's call, God speaks in a totally
different way, but it is still definitely haggadic. This man has
quite a different personality from Isaiah or Jeremiah, so God
speaks to him in a way that fits him. Ezekiel comes across as
a visionary and mystic with a lively imagination. So God uses
fascinating visions in Ezekiel's call to the prophetic ministry:
he is commanded to 'eat the scroll' (Ezekiel 3:1–3). In this
pictorial way it comes to Ezekiel that the Word of the Lord
needs to become part of him, and indeed to fill his whole
being. Likewise, the book ends with a fantastic vision of the
heavenly city representing the final glory of God's kingdom.
Before those final chapters we read the well-known story of
the prophet being taken into a valley with masses of dry bones
(Ezekiel 37). Just as in Genesis 2:7 God breathed into the dust
of the earth to form living human beings, so also God breathes
into the dry bones to restore them to life. Through this vision
God is teaching how his Spirit brings new life, a truth which
will come to its flowering in the glory of the resurrection of
Jesus and his gift of the Holy Spirit.

In the development of Ezekiel's prophecy he sees the
glory of God moving gradually away from its place above
the cherubim in the temple. It retreats to the threshold of the
temple (Ezekiel 9:3; 10:4) and then out of Jerusalem altogether

into the mountains (11:23). Through this, God is teaching his people the consequence of sin which separates us from God's glory. But later God promises that he will display his glory 'among the nations' (39:21) and thus Israel too will 'know that I am the LORD their God'. Finally, as part of the prophet's vision of the heavenly city, the glory of God returns and fills the temple (43:5; 44:4).

So God's truth is taught through these pictorial visions. But it should also be noted that such haggadic forms are occasionally accompanied even in Ezekiel by straight teaching of a more halachic nature. The two go hand in hand, but it is the visionary, the pictorial story-form teaching which stands out. In our witness and Bible teaching today we also need particularly to learn to teach in haggadic form.

Other prophets

Haggadah and pictorial storytelling play a vital part in the teaching of the other prophets. Visual teaching of this sort inspires and encourages.

The great stories of the book of Daniel are deeply significant in forming the spiritual instruction of Sunday school children all over the world. They thrill to the stories of Daniel's training at the royal court in Babylon, his interpreting the king's dream and, like Joseph before him, his promotion to the high position of ruler over the whole region. Children love to hear of Shadrach, Meshach and Abednego refusing to worship the king at the image of gold and being thrown into the fiery furnace; the mysterious hand writing the threatening words 'Mene, mene, tekel, parsin' on the wall before the king; the exciting story of the den of lions. These stories convey God's message to us all. What a faithful God he is! Finally, the closing chapters of the book contain dreams and visions which are replete with teaching, showing us God's control of the future as the God of history.

The life of Hosea is in itself a form of illustrated teaching concerning God's love for sinners. God commands the prophet to marry an adulterous woman who plays fast and loose in unfaithfulness, and leaves him to go back to prostitution. Hosea is then told to buy her back from prostitution and live with her again. The very names of her children also reveal the reality of God's judgment. The first child is named Lo-Ruhamah, meaning 'not loved', and her second child is Lo-Ammi, 'not my people'. Through Hosea's relationship with his adulterous wife Gomer and through the names of their children, God teaches about his redeeming love for us despite our appalling sinfulness. The seriousness of our sin comes across relentlessly, as does also the amazing grace and love of God. God's message is channelled through the story of Hosea, which is like a living parable. The story speaks for itself and needs little abstract theological teaching.

In Hosea the narrative seems totally adequate in conveying these fundamental truths, but less pictorial halachic teaching follows and further underlines their message. We could go through each of the Minor Prophets, observing the pictorial and narrative-style teaching in them: Joel's army of locusts, Amos's agricultural imagery, Jonah and the whale.

Like Ezekiel, the prophecies of Zechariah also come across through visions of a man among myrtle trees, four horns with craftsmen, the dress of the high priest, a golden lampstand with two olive trees, a flying scroll, a woman in a basket, and other such pictorial means of teaching God's Word.

The impact of the living story

It is the fascinating stories and other visual imagery that makes the Old Testament such a memorable and exciting series of books. Although this is mixed in with much abstract legal and theoretical instruction, it challenges our traditional ways of teaching theology, biblical exposition and communication of the gospel. Stories capture people's hearts and minds.

On my first ever visit to South Africa I saw the way one can capture someone's interest through using the living story of one's own personal experience.

I was flying from Johannesburg to Cape Town and found myself sitting next to a white man with a hard-bitten face. I tried to engage him in conversation and asked, 'Where are you going to? Cape Town?' Without any sign of interest he then asked me where I was going. I duly informed him that I too was going to Cape Town. It was of course the only place our flight was going to! Small talk on a plane can be amusingly ridiculous! But we immediately noticed that our answers were different in character. He grimaced with displeasure as he told me that he was going to Cape Town, whereas I sounded enthusiastic about the prospect of being in that beautiful city for the first time in my life.

He then explained that he was in the meat-canning business and had to visit a factory in Cape Town every few months. 'I don't enjoy these visits,' he continued. 'They are rather lonely affairs. When I get to the airport, there will be no-one to meet me. I will just take a taxi on my own to my hotel, go to my bedroom on my own, have dinner on my own, spend the evening on my own and go to bed by myself. Then tomorrow I will be on my own getting up, having breakfast, taking a taxi to the factory where we will talk about meat, tins and money.' Then he continued with this litany of loneliness as he recounted the same story of going back to the hotel and back again to the factory day after day.

'Happily it will not be like that for me,' I commented. 'I'm so looking forward to seeing Cape Town and I shall be met at the airport by a brother of mine. I so look forward to meeting him, because I've never met him before.' He looked surprised that I had a brother whom I had never previously met. Without explaining, I went on to talk of the fact that in my work I travel widely and enjoy meeting with family wherever I go. I talked of staying with a brother in Kabul, a sister in Buenos Aires, a brother in Moscow and another in Tokyo. 'So I rarely have to stay in hotels as I'm usually welcomed into the home of a brother or sister wherever I go,' I told this businessman. His eyes were beginning to come out on stalks.

'It must be amazing to belong to such a big widespread family,' he exclaimed. This allowed me to explain that, as a Christian, all other believers in Jesus are my sisters and brothers. We belong to one large loving family, so I have family wherever I go. I then explained to him how he could get into the family and gave him addresses of potential sisters and brothers both in Cape Town and Johannesburg. For a travelling businessman – and for an itinerant preacher! – the reality of the Christian church is indeed good news. Through the story of my own personal experience, the truth of the doctrine of the church became very relevant and interesting to a lonely businessman.

The New Testament

At first glance it appears that the New Testament is clearly divided between Halachah and Haggadah, between theoretical and legal teaching on the one hand and the historical story-form books on the other hand. The Gospels and Acts fit easily into the bracket of narrative teaching, and the book of Revelation adds its prophetic visions. But the Epistles seem to contain plain theological truth with straight moral application.

In fact, however, we find that the stories of the Gospels and Acts are interspersed with more theoretical teaching, while the theological content of the Epistles is interlaced with parables, pictorial and story-form application.

We may discern this combination of colourful stories with solid spiritual theory particularly clearly in John's Gospel. John recounts the story of one dramatic action after another. Each one is followed by a passage of verbal teaching of a more theoretical nature. And in the climax of his Gospel John presents us with a 'sign sandwich'. The great word of chapters 14 – 17 is bracketed by the visual action of the washing of feet beforehand, and by the cross and resurrection after it. Through his Gospel John has the repeated pattern of Deed + Word, but the glorious climax has Deed + Word + Deed.

Although Luke's two books teach largely through the stories of Jesus and the apostles, he also gives us more theoretical teaching in his version of the Beatitudes (Luke 6:20–26). But we note that this short passage is very much the exception in Luke's Gospel. Generally Jesus' teaching is communicated through historical events, parables or pictorial examples. In Acts, however, we do get the record of apostolic sermons which have some less visual teaching alongside what is richly pictorial. But again it is the record of the apostles' actions which are Luke's main means of teaching.

Matthew too is full of stories that speak for themselves. He is clearly writing for a Jewish church in times when most Jews were rejecting Jesus as Messiah and Lord. In this minority situation they needed encouragement with a reassurance that Jesus really is the eagerly awaited Messiah with God's complete authority. After the preparatory chapters with the birth stories, therefore, Matthew proceeds to show that Jesus has authority in his teaching. This comes across through the Sermon on the Mount, in which it is stressed that Jesus has a greater authority than all previous teachers – 'You have heard that it was said . . . But I tell you' (5:21–22, 33–34, 38–39, 43–44). Matthew summarizes the Sermon on the Mount with the declaration that 'the crowds were amazed at his teaching, because he taught as one who had authority' (7:28–29).

Jesus has such authority because it is in Jesus that the kingdom of God has come. He is the King of the kingdom and he has total authority. This should encourage that Jewish church that they are right to be following Jesus.

Following the Sermon on the Mount with its reassurance that Jesus has authority in his verbal teaching, Matthew tells the stories of a series of miraculous acts. Jesus heals a man with leprosy, the centurion's servant, a paralytic man and many others; he shows his power over the wind and waves and delivers two demon-possessed men; he gives life to a dead girl, sight to the blind and speech to the mute (8:1 – 9:34). Jesus has authority in active deed as well as in verbal teaching. He really *is* worth following – these stories demonstrate it!

This section is followed by chapter 10 in which Jesus calls his disciples to him and '[gives] them authority'. Not only does he have the authority to call disciples and send them out in mission, but he also passes on to them his authority. So Matthew's Gospel's concluding command to 'go and make disciples of all nations' is undergirded with the confident assurance that Jesus has all authority both in heaven and on earth (28:18–20). It is not easy here to distinguish between Halachah and Haggadah. The Sermon on the Mount has a mixture of both. Likewise, the final mission command comes through an active story of Jesus sending his disciples out in mission.

In his teaching on the kingdom, Jesus uses vivid parables (chapter 13). And in his feeding of the Jewish crowd, the so-called '5,000', and then his feeding of a Gentile crowd of 4,000 men (not counting women and children), he demonstrates his vision for mission both to Jews and Gentiles, not just to Israel as in the Old Testament. At that time it was expected that the Messiah would feed people of all nations in the messianic banquet at the table of Abraham. So Jesus' feeding of both Jewish and Gentile crowds enacted a messianic sign.

In any case, we may observe again how Matthew does not give any theoretical explanation of the feeding of the crowds. With Jewish readers the stories speak for themselves. He also does not make a point of explaining that one crowd consisted of Jewish people while the other one was in a Gentile area. His audience would see immediately the messianic significance. The kingdom of God relates not only to Jews, but also internationally to Gentiles of every nation.

The Gospels give us an ideal model of how to communicate Christian truth. Their captivating combination of actual historical fact, parables, quick pictorial imagery and lively vocabulary evokes living impressions in our minds. This brilliant style of teaching adds to the actual content to make the Gospels gripping to all sorts of people. Top academics still, after 2,000 years, are stimulated by their struggle to understand the deeper meaning of the New Testament. At the same time, unsophisticated tribal people and those with little education rejoice when they read the Bible, and they share its message without inhibition with their neighbours.

The Epistles

If the Gospels teach largely through historical and parabolic stories, the Epistles consist mainly of direct teaching on Christian truth and its implications for our lives. But just as the stories of the Gospels are intermixed from time to time with some more abstract teaching, so the Epistles use visual examples and historical narrative to illustrate the teaching.

So Paul, in his teaching on justification by faith rather than by obedience to the Jewish Torah (law), demonstrates his teaching through the historical stories of Abraham (Romans 4; Galatians 3:15–29), and Hagar and Sarah (Galatians 4:21 – 5:1). He also uses the story of Adam and the fall in his teaching concerning our new life in Christ (Romans 5:14). In Romans 11:13–24, Paul illustrates his theme of the universal validity of the gospel in the picture of dough penetrating 'the whole batch', and the well-known imagery of the olive tree of Israel with Gentile branches being added to the remnant Jewish branches.

Paul continually makes use of miniature stories of laying foundations and then building on them, kings and their rule, soldiers and their discipline. Although Jews and Muslims today may find it difficult to accept because of their long history of suffering through Christian violence, Paul even adopts military vocabulary to evoke illustrative pictures. As Christians today we are challenged to ask whether the words we use will conjure up the true biblical truths we long to share with the world.

When one reads Paul's letters, they seem to differ radically from the often dry theory of our Western theological works. Paul's writings abound in vivid forms of teaching which rivet our attention. In our contemporary globalized world we may find that Christians from Africa, Asia and Latin America will help us all to express ourselves in this more imaginative way. For example, even the titles of books by the Japanese K. Koyama differ radically from most Western theological works – *Waterbuffalo Theology, Mount Fuji and Mount Sinai, Three Mile an Hour God, No Handle on the Cross*.

In his epistle, the very Jewish James also uses short illustrative stories to make his teaching come alive. He talks of waves of the sea being tossed by the wind (James 1:6), the sun scorching plants with its heat (1:10–11), Abraham being called 'God's friend' (2:23), putting a bit in horses' mouths, great ships being steered by small rudders, the power of our small tongues to corrupt our whole person, and a small spark setting fire to a huge forest (3:3–12). He asks the question whether fresh water and salt water can flow from the same spring, a fig tree bear olives or a grapevine produce figs (3:11–12). Indeed James concludes his letter with the story of Elijah praying that it would not rain and then later that the rain would come (5:17–18). What a model of vivid pictorial teaching!

In each of the New Testament letters we find much teaching through such stories and imagery alongside more abstract theoretical teaching. But even the abstract teaching is communicated in evocative language which often induces vivid pictures in the readers' minds. As Christians we need to follow the biblical pattern in the way we share our faith at every level – to children, in our witness with non-believers, in church meetings, and in our theological and biblical teaching and writing.

To work on:

- Try to think up stories you could use to explain some of the basic truths of the gospel; for example, sin, repentance, faith, salvation, new and eternal life, the gift of the Holy Spirit, the family life of the church, mission worldwide, Jesus' second coming.

5. USING BIBLE STORIES IN EVANGELISM

Denis and I were eagerly looking forward to a couple of days sharing the good news of Jesus in a Muslim Malay village which had never before been reached with the gospel. What a privilege it was to know that we were the first ever Christians to visit that South Thailand village. The excitement of such pioneer evangelism never wore off although we had both preached about Jesus in many villages where no Christian had ever witnessed before. At that time, evangelism in South Thailand seemed a million miles from witness in Britain, but in more recent years we have faced the pioneer nature of much of our mission in a British village or an urban housing estate. Many people in Britain today know almost nothing of the Christian gospel or the teaching of the Bible. Of course the cultures of Britain and South Thailand are very different, but many of the principles of mission are similar.

'The people in our neighbourhood show little response to the good news of Jesus,' declared one minister to me, 'so we have to work extra hard in visiting around their homes, and in the pubs and local clubs. In an easier suburban area you can get away with a somewhat slacker ministry, but without really hard work and long hours nothing will happen in this area. The church will just remain minuscule, and stagnate.' In the relatively unresponsive context of Britain today it is easy for us all to shrug our shoulders and give up on witness. But God's call to share his good news comes to us afresh. Obedience to the Lord's command to proclaim his gospel demands not only hard work, but also much persevering faith and love.

Hard work lay before us too that afternoon in Thailand, as we thought ahead to the first meeting in the evening. We needed to advertise widely, so that the crowds would gather to hear God's message. Later, when we returned to Britain, we realized again that widespread pre-evangelism is vitally important before the gospel can make any significant impression on society. As we distribute Christian literature and advertise our message widely, one or two individuals may begin to come out of the woodwork to enquire about the good news of Jesus.

Fortunately we had been able to make use of an old-fashioned loudspeaker with a large trumpet-like metal megaphone. We agreed that we would cycle through the countryside from village to village with this megaphone, holding it in one hand while directing our bicycle with the other. We took it in turns to hold the megaphone while the other person carried the heavy bulk of the instrument.

The wet paddies of bright-green rice plants glinted in the hot tropical sun as we cycled precariously along the narrow raised boundaries between the fields. The relentless sun beat down on us, making the long ride even harder. And the regular daily tropical downpour of rain meant that the way was still slippery with treacherous mud. Cycling with just one hand, while carrying the megaphone in the other, made life difficult. Of course, if we slipped, we would find ourselves sprawling in the muddy water, and become objects of ridicule to everyone watching.

> Jesus loves me, this I know,
> for the Bible tells me so . . .

Someone had translated this Sunday school ditty into the local Malay language. It was the only easily accessible Christian song in that dialect, so we had little choice. Feeling how ridiculous we were, we laughed as we cycled through the little villages and the surrounding rice fields. Whichever of us held the trumpet-shaped loudspeaker sang at the top of his voice, so the countryside seemed to be filled with his singing! Soon crowds of children and a few adults began to follow us.

'The Pied Piper of Hamlin has nothing on us!' we quipped as we saw the growing crowds of children running in our wake.

We must have presented an amazing sight. Normally the villagers would never encounter white people, let alone seeing us with our one-handed precarious cycling and hearing our singing sounding across the rice fields. We certainly aroused their curiosity and they flocked to see us! Even a huge 6-foot-long monitor lizard looked up with evident interest from under the nearby trees.

Having drawn the crowds with our singing, we began to advertise the actual meeting.

'Come tonight to view the amazing film of the prophet Noah and his world-shattering flood!'

As Muslims, the local people believed in Noah as a prophet and they knew that he had survived a great flood, but no-one had ever told them further details of the story. We looked forward to filling in the gaps in their understanding. Why had God sent the flood and how had Noah survived it? What boat-building preparations had God commanded? What was done to ensure the survival too of the various animals? What members of his family had entered the ark with Noah and his wife? What happened when the flood subsided? What promises did God give with the visible sign of the rainbow? Such details of the story would fascinate the crowds. Even in our more sophisticated societies in Europe, the story of Noah captures people's attention and communicates great truths.

Recently I joined the cluster of people waiting for a bus. It had rained and a beautiful double rainbow arched above the end of the road. A woman excitedly took a photo. What an opportunity for me to tell them the story of Noah! 'What a beautiful rainbow, isn't it? I always think the story of how rainbows first started is really fascinating.' The little knot of people waiting for the bus began to listen attentively. It had never occurred to them that rainbows had not always just been part of nature.

'Yes, a man was told that there were going to be tremendous floods. To the amusement of everyone around, he built himself a large boat. Then he even started to move into the boat and live in it. He persuaded most of his family and local relatives to join him and even brought a whole lot of animals in too. "Why has he built that boat? He must be crazy – the sea is miles away!" they sneered.

'And then it began to rain. And it *did* rain! It was like a tremendous typhoon, and the floods began to rise until the whole area was badly flooded. The man's neighbours all drowned, and everywhere seemed to be more and more under the water. It was a national disaster. But after a while the floods receded and the sun began to shine again. Noah and his family got out of the boat, and God gave them the first rainbow together with the promise that he would never again destroy the world in spite of everyone's corruption and evil.'

The mention of the name 'Noah' and the introduction of God into the story made people aware that this was in fact a biblical story. If they had known from the start that the story came from the Bible, they would have switched off. Some probably reacted negatively when they discovered that the story was actually religious, but by then the bus was coming! Others may have started thinking about God's hatred of sin and his judgment, but God's merciful grace may also have come into their minds. Hopefully, rainbows began to have spiritual meaning to those people, and God would again show his grace through the sign of rainbows.

Of course in South Thailand too we aimed to show the biblical application of the whole event. We would apply the story of Noah, the flood, the ark and the rainbow to the truths of the gospel. Here was a picture of Jesus' atoning death and life-giving resurrection. Just as Noah found security and safety in the ark, so we today can find in Jesus salvation from all the threats of evil spirits, sin and the judgment. With the ever-increasing occultism and corruption in Britain today, the story of Noah has become vitally relevant. We long for the multitudes of our population to become aware of God's amazing grace.

Sadly, the story of Noah's salvation from the flood leads immediately to him falling into the sin of drunkenness (Genesis 9:20–23). In spite of all God's loving provision of salvation for Noah, sin continued to plague the world. In our society in Britain and also very much in student circles, drunkenness is a major problem. Our need of God's gracious gift of cleansing from sin and of life-transforming safety in

Jesus continues. As Christians we also know the reality of the Holy Spirit working within us to deliver us more and more from the power of sin.

So we finally arrived at the village and began to prepare for the evening meeting. In those days our equipment was basic in the extreme. We had no projector, but Denis had brilliantly converted a large torch into something that could show a film-strip. We also had no screen, but brought with us a big white sheet onto which to project our 'movie'. This was actually just an old filmstrip which gave the story of Noah without words, so we had to provide the commentary.

We had prepared carefully, knowing the importance of making Bible stories come alive. We had learned a wide variety of interesting expressions and words in the local language and had tried to foresee what questions and dis-cussions might arise. Even in our own language, storytelling needs careful preparation and vivid vocabulary to make our stories truly enthralling.

In the centre of the village was quite a large open space which would be ideal for the crowds who would gather to see the entertainment that evening. In front of it stood a rather tumbledown old house. Its windows were firmly shuttered and the door was obviously locked. It looked derelict and uninhabited. We noted immediately that this would be ideal for our 'screen'.

'Is this house empty?' we asked some of the young people. On hearing that it was indeed unoccupied, we asked about pinning our sheet to its wall as the screen for the film. Eagerly the young people nodded their heads. So we duly spread the white sheet across the house wall and over its front door. Having dealt with that, we could give our attention to fixing up the projector.

'The crowds are gathering,' we noted to each other with

satisfaction. 'And they seem to be watching everything with tremendous anticipation.'

Then the sheet began to bulge. Someone was trying to open their front door, but hit up against our sheet. After a moment or two an old woman poked her head round the end of the sheet! And the crowd burst out with laughter and cheering!

We had misread the reason behind their eager anticipation! Now we faced the battle to laugh with the young people, apologize to the embarrassed old woman, and try to recover control of the situation. Finally we were able to win everyone's rapt attention as we showed our filmstrip and recounted the story of Noah. How glad we were that the biblical account is so graphic and fascinating.

As evangelist in the mission hospital, I was accustomed to telling Bible stories every day of the week. I would spend the whole morning with the outpatients, sharing the good news of Jesus with one after another. A missionary nurse in the hospital had painted for me a series of pictures illustrating the story of Jesus healing the paralytic man (Mark 2:1–12). Sometimes I showed these pictures just to one patient alone; at other times a whole group would gather round me to hear the story. They loved Ann's pictures, but it was really the story that drew them. They could so easily picture the scene of Jesus being surrounded by such a crowd of listeners that the house was bulging with people. They were themselves patients and suffering from some sort of sickness, so they could readily feel sympathy with the paralytic. If they had known of someone with the power to heal diseases, they too would have hurried to find him. But then one could almost feel their disappointment when the paralytic and his friends were frustrated by the crowds surrounding Jesus. They could not get near him. What should they do? They were desperate to meet Jesus. My audience would laugh with delight at the thought of climbing onto the roof, making a hole and letting the sick man on his mat down through the opening. There was an eager sense of anticipation as they thought of Jesus' reactions. Would he rebuke the sick man for damaging the house? Would he say that he was too busy to help him now? Were the man's friends being too presumptuous in just presenting themselves to Jesus without any invitation? Western audiences often add another question: 'Can Jesus heal people today?'

Visiting a hospital in Britain today offers ideal opportunities for telling stories to the people sitting next to us. Waiting to see a doctor tests our patience, and a story from us can help pass the time. An initial question can prepare the way for a story – 'Did you hear about the man suffering from severe paralysis?' Depending on what sort of people are sitting next to us and what sort of conversation we have already had with them, the story can be told without hiding its biblical origin and the role of Jesus in it. But one can also change its details to fit an English hospital context. The unfortunate man with paralysis sat for hour after hour in the waiting room, but there were crowds of other people who were before him in the waiting list. His friends who had brought him to the hospital lost patience and forced their way into the doctor's room without being called. What a shock to the doctor and irritation among the other patients! How would the doctor react? At that stage we can tell people that a similar event is recounted in the Bible, but it was Jesus who gave the paralytic an amazingly gracious welcome and healed him with the words, 'Your sins are forgiven.' In secular Britain it is wise to keep the New Testament comment very brief unless we are asked to explain it. It may even be wise not to say that our story happened to Jesus, but merely to end with words like 'Wouldn't it be amazing if we could have God as our doctor?'

The Muslim patients in Thailand were always amazed and questioning when they heard Jesus' words to the paralytic: 'Son, your sins are forgiven.' How wonderful to have one's sins forgiven like that! But even Mohammed cannot forgive people's sins, so is it really true that Jesus has this glorious right to forgive sin? How can he do that? Only God has that ability, so is Jesus somehow equal with God? But to a Muslim that is blasphemy!

Questions flowed from their lips. The door was open for a declaration of the good news of who Jesus is, what he has done for us and what we need to do in response. As I counsel people, it becomes evident that a deep sense of guilt underlies most pastoral problems. People may not like to talk about 'sin', but guilt stalks our streets.

Relevant telling of Bible stories has enormous power in Muslim contexts, as in the rest of the world. In contemporary Britain too there is a sad ignorance of the Bible and its fascinating stories which can grip the attention not only of children, but also of students and other adults. In recent years, members of Christian Unions in Britain have distributed copies of a Gospel among their fellow students. Distributing New Testaments and offering to read them with our friends is something anyone can do. It is an easy way of witnessing. Many in Britain have never before read a Gospel and are fascinated by the brilliant stories they discover. Often they had assumed that a religious book like the Bible would be boring, old-fashioned and irrelevant. The Gospel stories soon show them the false nature of their prejudice. Perhaps Jesus does have something to give us which might heal some of our problems?

In earlier years of mission history, so-called 'tracts' consisted exclusively of a passage of Scripture. It was common to have tracts with a couple of biblical parables or one of Jesus' miracles. When I was in South Thailand we used a tract with the New Testament account of the healing of a man with leprosy. This was then a common disease in Thailand, so people knew well the ravages leprosy can inflict on a sufferer. Everyone feared the possibility that one day they might experience the symptoms – a white patch of skin, an area of the body with no sensation, perhaps already the fingers curling inwards. In the hospital we always had several leprosy patients, so it was very relevant to tell the story of Jesus healing someone with that horrendous disease. In the middle of the morning we would have a service in each ward and some-times we would tell that story. Almost every morning in each ward we would choose one of Jesus' parables or miracles for the talk. We often noticed how the patients responded so feelingly to biblical stories whereas they merely listened politely when we preached without telling a Bible story.

In the afternoons and evenings I visited the wards, chatting with the patients and their families. Sometimes they would ask me to tell them again the story we had used in the morning services. This gave me the further opportunity of showing them the story in the New Testament and giving them a copy of the relevant Gospel. Then they could read the story of Jesus for themselves. We prayed that the stories of the Gospels would draw people to Jesus in loving faith. We longed for them to see that Jesus stands head and shoulders above all others. He alone is the Lord, the Saviour, the Redeemer, God incarnate as one of us. No other religious prophet or leader can deal with sin and evil. His cross and resurrection stand out as brilliantly unique. But the theological implications of the biblical stories would not come right away. Before that, people would come to admire and love Jesus. It was only later that they began to formulate the truths which lay behind their experience of what Jesus did for them and indeed for all who follow him.

On Fridays, the key day for Muslims, I cycled away from the hospital in order to visit a few surrounding villages and preach there. Again and again people would recognize me as coming from the hospital. Often they would ask me to tell again the stories they had heard while there. So our Bible stories spread around the whole region. How people love stories – and the biblical stories are so fascinating!

In more recent years it has been my privilege to be the speaker in many Christian conferences both in Britain and overseas. Several times I have noted that one of the optional seminars was on storytelling. With keen anticipation of gaining new insights into the subject, I often chose that particular seminar to attend. To my disappointment, however, these seminars commonly restricted themselves to the topic of telling biblical stories interestingly. This is of course vitally important and may be the first step in storytelling. But I had hoped that they would also discuss cross-cultural story-telling: how to tell Christian stories, for example, to people of a different generation or educational level. And in our globalized world, we need to learn how to tell stories within a Muslim, Jewish, Hindu or Buddhist culture. Although, of course, it is vitally important that we make the biblical stories come alive, I was disappointed that the seminars did not relate the stories cross-culturally.

It is nothing new to want to make Bible stories come alive. Sunday school teachers have always worked hard to make their teaching lively for the children. Parents, aunts and uncles may have given less thought to it, but unconsciously they too work to fascinate their children when they tell them Bible stories at bedtime. For cross-cultural mission workers, this is a difficult but very rewarding task, as they grapple with a foreign language in another religious and social context.

When we were working in the churches of North Sumatra in Indonesia, training for baptism was based on an old book called *104 Bible Stories*. The book itself failed miserably to bring the stories to life, but those teaching the baptism courses made every effort to make them interesting.

One of the local church elders was particularly brilliant in teaching biblical stories with amazing vitality. On one occasion he described Isaiah's words of judgment against the women of Zion (Isaiah 3:16–24). His eyes flashed below his curly black hair as he described the women 'tripping along with mincing steps, with ornaments jingling on their ankles'. Of course the prophet's words are in themselves hugely descriptive, but the way it was taught was unforgettable.

My wife remembers this elder teaching the story of Noah. Again, the actual story in the Bible is in itself wonderfully gripping. But she has never forgotten his rendering. His expressive face reflected the flashing lightning and frightening thunder. God's message penetrates our hearts and minds when the biblical stories are told well. Let us not neutralize the brilliance of these stories by boring presentation.

Like a good actor, we need to enter into the feel of the whole story and its characters. We will change the sound of our voice to fit the different people in the story. We may lower our voices where the plot becomes more sinister or threatening. And our words will flow excitedly and more rapidly when the tension rises. Our gesticulations and facial expressions will add colour and make the story even more vivid. Beware an unemotional deadpan expression on the face and a flat monotonous voice! Purposefully chosen pauses can add to the suspense. Be as joyfully uninhibited as you can when you are telling a story!

The film industry has discovered the excitement of one or two of the biblical stories. For example, the story of Moses was told in an epic film which became a box office hit. The film brought out the dynamic of the Old Testament history and drew millions of people into the cinemas of the world. Various films have also portrayed the life of Jesus, and the so-called 'Jesus Film' has captivated hearts all over the world.

Questions:

- How can we encourage people in our church to be involved and work hard to witness in our community?
- Can you think of an ordinary everyday situation in your life where there might be an opportunity to share a story which points people to Jesus?

6. ADAPTING OTHER PEOPLE'S STORIES

Knowing that I have taught courses on storytelling, sometimes people ask me to think up a new story on a particular subject. When this happens, I am always lost for words. I have never learned to invent stories myself. In my career as a storyteller I have always taken over other people's stories, but adjusted them for a different cultural and religious context. But in my courses I have been excited at the brilliance of my students in thinking up great stories to illustrate biblical truths.

What, then, was my way forward after hearing Dr Gordon Gray's penetrating words: 'If we want to communicate effectively with Malay Muslims, we shall have to learn to tell stories'?

Of course I would continue to use Bible stories, especially those which showed the beauty and glory of Jesus. But I needed more than that. When preaching in the open air I needed stories which would hold a crowd of Muslim men for at least half an hour.[5] Ordinary preaching intrigued a handful of men for a short time, but after ten or fifteen minutes they would begin to lose interest and drift away.

My mind turned to Dr Paul White's brilliant series of Jungle Doctor books. As a flying doctor in East Africa, he was writing in a context which was a bit different from Thailand. And his audience came from an African tribal religious background, while the great need in South Thailand was to reach Asian Muslims with the good news of Jesus. But the Jungle Doctor stories were fascinating and could surely be adapted for a different cultural and religious context. In Britain too they can be used to great effect. It is wonderful to watch people's faces when one asks, 'Have you heard the story of . . . ?' and then tell the story itself. British people thoroughly enjoy these stories with little or no adaptation for modern European life. The application will need to be changed slightly, but not the story itself.

I had only been in Asia for about a year, so my language was still somewhat inadequate. Telling stories requires considerable width of expression and vocabulary if it is to grip an audience. It seemed right, therefore, to restrict my repertoire to just two stories. Having chosen them, I worked hard with a language teacher. It was encouraging to see how much he enjoyed working with me on those stories. He entered into the heart of them and thought up all sorts of interesting ways to make them come alive. He suggested ways of stimulating repartee. He foresaw the questions which might arise from within the audience and helped me to formulate good answers. For missionaries and storytellers a good language teacher can prove invaluable!

Soon the day came when the first story was ready and I was able to gather a small crowd of Muslim men. As I told the story, it soon became evident that those men so enjoyed the story that they stayed with me. And bit by bit others joined until several hundred men stood before me in a large open space. Afterwards they scattered and retold my story to their families and neighbours, so it spread widely.

Be sure your sin will find you out! (Numbers 32:23)

Once upon a time in a far-off village there was a young boy who proudly owned a much-loved hen. Early each morning his hen would lay a fresh egg and with pride would let out a triumphant call (in telling the story one can imitate a hen crowing after laying an egg!). Each morning, therefore, a beautiful fresh egg lay in the hen house waiting for the boy to come and collect it.

Now, near the hen house a young snake lived with his father snake in a pile of wood. Each morning they heard the hen's call, and the young snake could not resist the temptation. He knew that the fresh egg would taste so delicious. One morning the young snake went to explore the hen house and found that there was a convenient little hole at the bottom of one wall. 'I could get into that shed without too much trouble,' the little snake thought to himself.

So the young snake shared with his father how he intended to get hold of the newly laid egg in that hen house.

'Be careful, little snake,' the father snake warned. 'Stealing people's eggs can lead you into untold danger.'

The little snake saw no need to heed his father's warning. He had seen how easy it would be to get into that hen house and steal the egg. 'Neither the boy nor his father will be awake so early in the morning,' he thought. 'My dad is far too careful. There won't be any danger. And I shall enjoy that egg!'

(In a village context there would often be considerable repartee about snakes stealing eggs and even killing hens, so that added to the interest.)

The next morning the hen duly laid a lovely fresh egg and crowed with proud delight. The boy heard it, and half asleep he pictured the egg he would fetch from the shed when he got up. But meanwhile the young snake was wide awake and ready to go. With his father's words of warning ringing in his ears, the snake made his way to the hen house, came to the narrow hole and just managed to get through it. He soon found the fresh egg and swallowed it with greedy anticipation. The egg slid down his body, forming a bulge where it finally lodged. Then the snake went back to the hole in the wall. But with the egg bulging in his stomach, he couldn't get through the hole. So he wriggled and wriggled and wriggled his tummy (the crowds enjoyed me showing how one can wriggle one's tummy!) until finally the egg broke, spilling its fresh warm contents deliciously in his stomach. (Here the story-teller can show the sense of delight in his/her facial expression while rubbing the stomach!) Now that the little snake's body no longer protruded in the middle, he happily succeeded in getting through the hole and safely back home.

Later in the morning the boy got up and made a beeline to the shed to get the expected egg. But no egg was to be found. He searched the whole shed, but still no egg!

For several days this was repeated. The hen laid her egg and crowed loudly, the snake stole the egg, couldn't get out through the hole, wriggled his tummy to break the egg, and escaped home safely. Each morning the boy went to get the egg and found none. Why was there no egg? The boy could not understand what was happening.

'I think there must be a snake stealing your eggs,' the boy's father suggested when his son shared his bewilderment. 'I know what we should do,' he declared firmly. 'We'll boil another egg for twenty minutes until it's rock hard. Then we'll go early to the shed and wait until your hen lays her egg.

We'll quickly take the freshly laid egg and replace it with our hard-boiled one.'

The next morning the little snake heard the hen's call and set off to get her egg. Once again the father snake warned his son to be careful, for stealing from people is dangerous. But the little snake thought he knew better and confidently set off for the shed. He duly swallowed the egg happily and began to find his way through the hole to escape. As usual, he wriggled his body in order to break the egg and enjoy the sensuous warmth of the fresh food in his stomach. Desperately he wriggled and wriggled and wriggled. But this time the egg would not break. With the bulge in his stomach the little snake was caught – he could neither go through the hole nor return backwards into the shed. So ended the life of that snake!

'Be sure that your sin will find you out' (Numbers 32:23). Every Muslim believes that we shall all be judged when we die. How can we escape the judgment of God and be accepted into paradise, the Holy Land? If our sin is not washed away, we shall not be able to enter paradise, that place of total purity. It is not enough just to say, 'God is merciful', the common Muslim answer. God will never allow people to enter heaven when their sin has not yet been dealt with and removed, for otherwise heaven will be contaminated by our sin.

Many questions and considerable debate can follow from this story. Of course the moral of the story must be differently applied with a British audience. In Britain today it is considered almost unacceptable to talk about judgment or hell. Even the word 'sin' may need to be replaced with 'evil' or 'corruption'. With the widespread infiltration of the Hindu and Buddhist concept of karma, the law of cause and effect, it may be good to apply this story by debating the rights and wrongs of karma. How does God's grace relate to the reality that our actions do have inevitable consequences? In any context this story can lead to some direct application and an explanation of the gospel, or one can leave people with their questions to allow the Holy Spirit quietly to continue working in them.

This story fits well into a Western context in Europe today. Owing to the subtle influence of existentialist New Age thought and postmodernism, spirituality has been separated from ethics and morality. In this context people can be very 'spiritual' without any attempt to live moral lives. But as Christians we worship the God of holiness and have within us the Spirit of holiness. This story of the little snake which is killed because of stealing the boy's eggs opens the door to good biblical teaching that God is looking for righteousness as the necessary consequence of a living relationship with him. He is a holy God who demands holiness. And evil always has dire consequences. Without righteousness there can only be God's judgment, and sorrow is the result. A parable like this makes it easier to teach unpalatable truths more acceptably.

Why Christmas?

'Come,' the farmer said to his much-loved pet monkey. 'It's time for us to plant our peanuts, so that we can have a good harvest later in the year. We shall then be able to feast on our peanuts and sell some to get money to buy other things.' So the farmer set out for his field with a spade over his shoulder, a bag of seed peanuts in his other hand, and the monkey walking quietly beside him (in the original Jungle Doctor story the farmer has a pet dog, but to Muslims dogs are unclean and it is not appropriate to have one as a pet).

On arrival at his field the farmer quickly got down to work. Early in the morning it was still relatively cool and pleasant to work. He knew that soon the sun would rise and burn inexorably upon him while he worked. Then the perspiration would flow down his body and his damp shirt would cling to him. 'We'll try to get the peanuts into the ground as quickly as possible. Then we can go home and relax in the midday heat.' He smiled as he thought of the pleasure of having a good day's work behind him and sitting in the shade at home with a cool drink.

He started by digging a shallow trench the whole length of the field. His monkey quietly followed him, and the farmer enjoyed the sense of companionship. He liked having the pet monkey with him. Happily he leaned over and gave the monkey a gentle caress. 'How like us humans monkeys are!' he thought and smiled with contentment.

Opening his seed bag, the farmer began at the beginning of the trench he had dug. He carefully began to plant the peanuts. Between them he allowed a space of about a foot to give the plants room to grow and yield a good harvest of peanuts from their roots. One peanut after another he planted. As he moved on to the next seed, he neatly covered up the previous one with the soil.

To his horror he turned round and saw his pet monkey following behind him, solemnly digging up the peanuts he had just planted and quietly eating them. The monkey was enjoying the feast. 'Surely he's putting the peanuts into the ground especially for me,' the monkey must have thought to himself.

'Please don't dig up my peanuts!' the farmer said gently to his monkey. 'You and I, we depend on these peanuts. If we don't get a good yield from them, we shall go hungry in days to come. So be a good monkey and leave the peanuts where I plant them,' he carefully explained. As he did so, he stroked the monkey caringly to show his appreciation of the companionship which his pet gave him day after day.

Then the farmer began his peanut planting all over again. He dug the trench again in preparation for planting. He again began to put the seed peanuts in, carefully leaving adequate space between each one. Finally he covered each one with the loose earth and pressed it down with his foot.

As he continued down the line with his planting, to his annoyance he saw that the monkey was again digging up the newly planted peanuts and enjoying eating them. Monkeys do like peanuts! Indeed peanuts are sometimes even called 'monkey nuts'. 'How can I explain to my monkey that he should leave the seeds in the ground and not eat them?' he wondered to himself. 'Last time I was nice and friendly to him, spoke nicely to him in a kind, gentle voice. And while explaining to him, I showed my love by stroking him in the way he most enjoys. But he obviously didn't understand what I meant. Being warmly kind and loving just doesn't work in asking my monkey not to eat my peanuts.'

The farmer thought to himself, 'Perhaps he will understand more readily if I show real anger at him digging up my peanuts.' So he hit his pet monkey several times and angrily shouted, 'Don't eat my peanuts! Bad monkey! I warn you, if you do that again, I will punish you really severely.' The monkey winced and cowered with obvious fear. Usually he had such a nice friendly relationship with his master. So he felt the weight of the angry words and the chastisement.

The farmer duly returned to the end of the field, digging up the trench all over again. Once more he carefully inserted the seed peanuts, covered them with the loose soil and firmed it down to give the peanuts the perfect conditions for their growth.

But as he proceeded down the line he noted with horror that once again the monkey was following behind him, digging up the peanuts and quietly eating them.

'What can I do to make my pet monkey understand that he shouldn't eat my peanuts?' he asked himself. 'I have tried being kind and nice with him, gently explaining it to him. I stroked him with obvious marks of my love for him. But it was all to no avail; he just didn't understand. And the temptation to eat those delicious peanuts was too great for him. Then I also tried being really angry with him and punished him severely for eating the peanuts. I spanked him with loud, angry words. I warned him that if he did it again, I would punish him even more severely. But still he didn't understand and happily ate my peanuts without any appreciation of what I told him.'

The farmer stopped and sat down under a tree to consider what he could do to make his pet monkey understand what he wanted.

In some despair he came to the realization that there was no possible way for him to speak effectively to the monkey. The only way to communicate to a monkey, he realized, is to become a monkey oneself. Then one can learn monkey language. Only in this way can a human being make a monkey understand what he wants and what is against his will.

Sadly, however, we mere human beings do not have the ability to become a monkey and so identify with the life and thought of a monkey. Because the farmer could never become a monkey, he had no way to communicate what he wanted to his pet.

In telling this story, one is already beginning to use more religious language as the story draws towards its conclusion. Already one is planting the seed-thought of whether perhaps God can do what is impossible for us humans. Can God indeed put aside the glory of his heavenly state and come down to earth to become a mere human being? In a Muslim society it is of course totally unacceptable to suggest that something might be beyond what God can do. But at the same time the thought that God could demean himself and take on human nature contradicts everything that Islam believes about God's greatness.

Like the farmer, God sometimes treats us with grace and loving kindness, pouring out his generous blessings. But even when God is so good to us, people may still ignore him and fail to follow his will for their lives. Sometimes, however, God may allow his judgment to show us his holiness and anger against sin. Even then, we often ignore God and go our own way without listening to the voice of God. The farmer too tried to get his message across to his much-loved pet monkey first through love and gentleness, then through angry punishment. But neither means proved effective.

This Jungle Doctor story may provoke strong debate and lively discussion among a Muslim audience. Questions may flow. And the answers can only lead to an explanation of the Christian faith. Most Muslims assume that Christians believe that the man Jesus somehow became God, but our story reverses this and teaches the true Christian belief that God became human.

To many Muslims this is absolutely unacceptable. To them it is so blasphemous that they may lose their temper with the Christian storyteller, and stones may begin to fly in his or her direction!

The story of the peanuts also raises the issue of whether God in his absolute glory still desires to communicate his will to us as human beings. Is God's word only to be found in the revealed scriptures of the Qur'an with the possible addition of the Hadith, the thoughts, words and deeds of Mohammed? Or does God want to form such a relationship with his followers that he can speak to us in ways that all of us can understand? As we noted before, elephants hardly even notice ants and certainly do not desire any communication with them. But is that an adequate picture of God? God is too *akbar* (great) to be defined with such examples.

With a bigger group it may well be better just to conclude with a couple of stimulating questions.

When I first used this story, it was in the Muslim context of South Thailand. But it relates equally well in the West or anywhere else. If we are teaching an Enquirers' Course it would be helpful in dealing with the topic of Jesus as God incarnate. Of course it does not explain *how* Jesus Christ is both fully human and at the same time fully divine. The theological debates of the early Christian centuries lie beyond the reach of this story. But even those Christians who recite the Creeds on a Sunday are unlikely to join battle with these Greek philosophical formulations. These matters can be by-passed in our evangelism.

At Christmas time, many Christians are hungry for new ways of explaining the well-known stories and truths of our Saviour's birth. This story of the farmer and his pet monkey could be told within the bosom of the family, in a Christmas party or in a church meeting. Through it people would learn that Christmas signifies God becoming a human being in order to forge a relationship with us and 'speak our language'.

Why Christmas? The Christmas story shows us God's unique way to teach people not to eat his peanuts!

All over the world different peoples treasure their ancient tales which often include one in which God is actively engaged in this world. Travelling through New Zealand on a coach tour, a friend of ours was introduced to a traditional Maori story. All the passengers listened enthralled as the tale unfolded.

Long, long ago the Great Spirit in the Sky made this world. It shone with abundant beauty, full of colour and light. All the animals delighted in the splendour of what the Great Spirit had made. Sadly, after some while, many dark and obnoxious insects began to multiply. They invaded the beautiful forests, leaving their filthy detritus everywhere. The longer they stayed, the darker and dirtier everything became. Finally all the light and beauty which the Great Spirit had made for the enjoyment of all creatures was despoiled. The Great Spirit could bear it no longer.

'Who will go for us and clear my world of all this dirt which is spoiling everything?' he asked. One animal after the other began to make excuses. They didn't want to get dirty through clearing up the mess.

Eventually the little kiwi bird came forward. His wings gleamed with iridescent colours as he flew across to the Great Spirit. 'I am willing to go,' he said. 'But what must I do?'

'Go into the forest,' the Great Spirit said. 'But are you sure you are willing to pay the cost? As you remove all the dirt, it will inevitably damage you. The brilliant colours of your wings will be covered with the black dirt. Living for so long under the leaves of the forest, you will lose your ability to fly. Ashamed of your dark and dirty appearance, you will only emerge at night.'

The kiwi bird thought long and hard. He hated to lose his beautiful colours and dreaded the prospect of never flying again. He felt sad at the thought of never walking in the light of day, but always haunting the dark.

Finally, however, he made his decision. 'I will do your work and be your servant in cleaning up the insects' mess,' he said.

And that is why today the inconspicuous kiwi has become the much-loved bird which has been taken to the heart of every New Zealander. In fact it has become the emblem of the 'Kiwis', the people of New Zealand, and also given its name to a delicious fruit which is now eaten all over the world.

So the redeeming work of the Suffering Servant foretold by Isaiah may be taught to people not only in New Zealand, but in any situation in any country. Stories can make biblical truth and theology come alive.

A challenge:

- Work on one of these stories and try telling it to a child, in your church or to a group of friends. You can start perhaps by telling them, 'I have just read about . . . Have you heard this story?'

7. TEACHING BY PARABLES

The postman came with a little bundle of letters. 'Look at this,' I exclaimed to Elizabeth, showing her a smartly official-looking envelope. We quickly noted that it came from the office of the Sultan of Johore in Malaysia.

'It has come to our attention that you are disturbing the peace of the State,' the letter inside declared baldly. It proceeded to inform us that we were required to attend a meeting with the head of police, the head of the ministry of religion and another high official.

We knew that it was illegal in Malaysia to witness to Muslims, but we had been working in Indonesia where religious freedom prevailed, according to the national consti-tution. We then came to work in Malaysia to pastor a young Chinese church. But I spoke Indonesian which is closely related to Malay, so I was naturally drawn to the Malay people who were Muslims. I felt too that no-one would worry too much about what I did. I was just an unknown young man working in a small market town. So I had felt free to share my faith openly with Malays in the town. I also distributed Gospel tracts in Malay with my name and address on the back, offering a free Gospel to anyone who wrote in.

I wondered with considerable anxiety what these top officials would say or do. I went to meet them with much prayer and nervousness. They put aside all formalities and got straight down to business. The interview was conducted in the Malay language, but I tried to avoid showing any sign of fluency in the language.

Having established the facts of the case, the officials delivered their ultimatum. They required me to promise not to take the initiative in witnessing about the Christian faith to Muslims. If I refused to give that promise, they informed me that I would be given twenty-four hours to leave the country – and this would apply also to all other members of the organization of which I was a member. At that time our organization had some seventy workers in Malaysia. In my mind I imagined future history books recording how their whole ministry among Chinese and Indians in Malaysia had come to an end because of me! On the other hand, Muslims represented at least half the total population of the country. Is it right before the Lord to promise not to witness to such a group of people? And I had the language skills for such witness. What turmoil raged within me! But I was not given the leisure to think quietly through the choice before me and to come before the Lord in prayer about it. The officials were seated on the other side of the large polished table, waiting for my answer.

Suddenly God's answer came. I remembered the words of Dr Gordon Gray and my experience with storytelling in Thailand. There was no need to take the initiative in witnessing. I could just tell stories without any mention of Jesus or the Bible, but the stories could act as pre-evangelism. They could prepare the ground for the seed of God's good news in Jesus Christ.

And so began a new stage in my ministry of storytelling.

In Thailand I had been an inexperienced new mission worker, having only been on the job for about a year. My Malay language skills had been barely adequate for telling stories effectively. Now we had served for a few years in Indonesia too and our Malay flowed freely. I felt more confident and could venture into new forms of storytelling. I began to use the parables of Jesus and give them a Muslim context, applying them in ways which related to a Muslim-background audience. It quickly became clear that the Muslim authorities were watching me carefully. From time to time men came to ask me questions about my faith, but I suspected that they were spying on me. But all was well; my stories were not apparently Christian in any way and could have been told quite acceptably even in the most conservative Muslim situation. But they opened the door to people asking vital questions about faith. This could lead people to discover Jesus as the unique answer to their needs.

Parables obviously fitted the situation among Muslims in Malaysia at that time. With such stories I could prepare the ground for Muslims to face the glorious gospel of Jesus without directly stating that my stories were Christian or that they came from the Bible. As in many countries in Asia and Africa, a storyteller is highly esteemed, so it was good to be known among the Muslim population as 'the storyteller'.

I was recently standing on the street corner in Platt, Manchester waiting to be picked up for a church meeting. Crowds of Muslims swirled past me together with a handful of Hindus and Sikhs. 'Platt is already largely Muslim,' my host commented, 'and one day it is very possible that it will become exclusively Muslim.' I realized that my experience among

Muslims in Asia was very appropriate for witness now in Britain. Telling the Christian faith through stories would relate perfectly with ethnic minorities here in Europe. Then I realized that actually ethnic English people would also enjoy stories very much.

'Did you hear about the millionaire Haji Aziz paying his zakat⁶ last year?' I asked the four other men in the taxi as we drove down to Singapore (cf. Jesus' story of the widow's offering in Mark 12:41-44 and Luke 21:1-4). Back in the 1960s the drive to Singapore took about an hour and a half. The road was lined with mile after mile of rubber estates. As a foreigner doing this journey it was at first quite interesting to observe the rubber trees with the latex dripping steadily into a cup below the freshly cut bark of the tree. But after doing the journey again and again every week, the interest turned into boredom. And local people had grown up in a country which was full of rubber estates, so the trip was for them doubly boring. How good therefore to be entertained by a story! Of course they did not realize that it was just a parable; they assumed that Haji Aziz was a real person and, like people all over the world, they were delighted to learn a bit of titillating gossip.

'The time has come for me to give you my annual zakat,' the haji informed the local Muslim leader over the phone. 'When would it suit you for me to come to your house and give you a cheque? As usual, I would like to give it to you personally face to face.'

The imam's smile of happy anticipation could almost be felt through the telephone. 'The mosque committee and I will be delighted to see you just whenever your diary will allow it.' So it was arranged for the coming Tuesday afternoon.

As the time approached, the haji faced a difficult question. Which car should he use? There was the gold-covered Rolls, the sleek-looking Jaguar or the business-like Mercedes. After some consideration he decided on the Rolls and instructed his chauffeur accordingly.

Meanwhile the imam was preparing for the haji's visit. He asked his wife to go and buy some of the best cakes and sweet-meats. But what should they drink? When on his own without anyone watching, he allowed himself the pleasure of some alcohol, and he knew that the haji and some on the mosque committee secretly went against Muslim law in this way. But on this occasion it did not seem wise or appropriate. He finally decided that hot chocolate would be best and asked his wife to prepare the best china for the visit.

As would be culturally expected, Haji Aziz arrived some ten minutes late. The imam and the mosque committee members were waiting for him and gave him a gracious welcome. One of them opened the door of the Rolls for him to get out. Smiles and Muslim handshakes and formal greetings followed.

All together they went into the imam's house and soon found themselves comfortably seated while the usual small talk and conversation ensued. The imam's wife and older daughter came in with the hot chocolate and cakes, discreetly serving them to each guest without a word.

At first the men politely ignored the food and drink on the tables before them. Then the conversation purposely slowed to allow the imam to take his drink into his hands and with a brief word of welcome invite them all to drink and eat. He himself gave the lead by taking a mouthful of the hot chocolate. Following his example, the others also took a small sip. Then after a while the imam again took his cup and this time had an ample drink, allowing the guests to feel free to eat and drink as they wanted.

Conversation flowed, but it was clear that everyone was eagerly awaiting the time when the millionaire would hand over what he had decided to give as his zakat. How much would he give? His money could transform the finances of the whole mosque, which needed repainting and funds for its social programme.

Finally the long-awaited moment came. The haji turned to the imam. 'May I break into our conversation and pass you my zakat cheque? Please excuse me breaking into such generous hospitality and pleasant conversation with the trifling matter of just a small cheque.'

'It is always an honour and pleasure to welcome you to our mean little home.' The haji spread his hands with a gesture of humility. 'We do apologize that we could not welcome you in a fashion more suited to you, but we give you a warm welcome.'

Everyone smiled politely, but their hearts were fixed on the haji's cheque. What would he write? How much would he give?

The chequebook emerged from his pocket with a flourish. It was slowly followed by a gold pen. After a tantalizing pause, the millionaire began to write. No-one dared to let it be seen that they were desperately trying to read what he wrote.

'Please excuse me that my zakat is only a trifling hundred thousand dollars,' the multimillionaire quietly announced. But what satisfaction he felt as he sensed how impressed they all were with his generosity! At the same time he thought to himself, 'Happily they are thrilled with my generosity, but a hundred thousand dollars won't make more than a tiny dent in my accounts.' With very real contentment he thought of the large sums of money which had flowed into his bank accounts in recent months and would still remain intact after this visit to the imam.

As I told the story in the taxi en route to Singapore, the other four passengers and the driver listened with greedy fascination as their thoughts circled round that huge sum of money.

'Now it just happened that the next day a poor beggar went to the mosque to give God a small gift,' I continued my story. He was very poor and his clothes were far from smart, but he realized that he had always had just enough to eat and had always been able to clothe himself. 'God has been amazingly merciful to me,' he mused.

So it was that he went to the mosque with a heartfelt sense of gratitude to God. In his pocket was a five-cent piece, which assured him of his next meal, but that was all he had. Feeling somewhat out of place, he entered the mosque. Quietly, when no-one was looking, he donated his one small coin.

'Which gift was more pleasing to God?' I would ask my Muslim audience. 'The multimillionaire's or the old beggar's?'

When telling this story more widely, reactions varied considerably. Some young men failed totally to answer the question, for they were dreaming covetously of the $100,000. To them my question was ridiculous. 'God isn't stupid!' they would laughingly exclaim. 'Which would you prefer? A hundred thousand dollars or five cents? You can't do anything with five cents, but a hundred thousand . . .'

Many traditional Muslims with no influence from outside Islam would assume that the large gift was better. With such money the mosque would be able to do many good things.

A few more open people realized that our motive in giving could be significant. This relates to the Muslim doctrine of *niyyah* (intention). Niyyah is commonly used to mean that someone intends to fulfil their religious duty later, although for some reason they cannot do it at the prescribed time. But niyyah can also signify one's *motive*.

Just occasionally, someone would come to me weeks or even months later with the serious question, 'How can I get a right motive in my giving or praying? Your story has been on my mind and I know that my motives are wrong. I pray and give just to follow my tradition and to show everyone that I am a good Muslim.' Although they didn't use the word 'repentance', I felt that such people were beginning to face the sinfulness of their hearts and desire God's saving work on their behalf.

If I was confident that the person was not a spy, I could then explain that as a Christian I believe that only Jesus by his Holy Spirit can change our hearts and give us truly godly motives. 'But as a Christian I am biased,' I would say. 'You are a Muslim and must first try to find an answer to your need within your own religion. If you can't find a solution to your question in Islam, come and see me again and I will explain more about the Christian way.' And one or two did come back to me.

It is important that Muslims should not be encouraged to put their faith in Jesus until they see that Islam cannot help them. Otherwise they are likely to succumb to the fearful pressures of persecution. Satan will whisper in their ears, 'You're a fool. Why did you leave Islam and follow that foreign religion? Now you are suffering for it. Just return to Islam, your own natural religion, and you can find everything you need there.' There can be no worse witness than someone who has professed conversion to Jesus Christ and then gone back to Islam. 'I tried Christianity,' they may testify, 'but it didn't work. Actually Islam gives us more than anything those Christians claim.' Such a testimony makes it doubly hard for that person to become a true Christian later and deters others too from following the Lord. I prefer therefore not to push people into a profession of faith too quickly. It is better that they only become Christians after they have become deeply aware that Islam cannot give them the fullness of salvation that Jesus offers us. When they are definitely disillusioned with

Islam, then they may continue with enduring perseverance as Christians when they face even violent persecution.

Jesus' parabolic teaching

'Why does the college library have all those books on Jesus' parables?' a Jewish student asked. 'Their meaning is so obvious,' she continued. Some cultures use parables in their teaching and so understand them quite easily. For other societies, parables represent an alien form of teaching which is not so easily understood. For a Jewish student the basic meaning of the parables seems rather obvious, while for others that may not be the case.

Actually, however, even Jesus' disciples found his parables hard to grasp, so they had to ask him what they meant. But Jesus was often surprised that they did not grasp the meaning of his parables. 'Are you so slow to understand?' he would ask them. On several occasions he gave them a full interpretation of some parable because they hadn't understood what he meant. Two thousand years later, Christians are still struggling to understand the full significance of his parables, although they seem outwardly to be such simple little stories.

'It's clever to be simple,' declared the Oxford lecturer on Pushkin, the father of Russian literature. 'But if you don't really know what you are talking about, wrap it up in clever academic language!' Jesus' parables are so delightfully simple. They not only use everyday language, but are based on the normal events of ordinary life.

No modern university would grant a doctorate for telling stories like Jesus' parables. 'There was a man with a hundred sheep . . .'; 'One man built his house on the rock, while another man built his on sand . . .'; 'A Jewish man was severely hurt by bandits, but the priest and the Levite passed by on the other side without helping him. A Samaritan however . . .' No student today could offer such stories in the academic world. But those parables still speak today 2,000 years after Jesus told them. They may be simple, but they are not simplistic.

'Why do you speak to the people in parables?' the disciples asked Jesus. Such a pertinent question! Why did he not just speak clearly so that everyone would understand his message? We have already observed that stories and parables have particular power in communication. But Jesus gave another reason for his use of parables.

While Jesus wanted his own followers to learn from him and understand his teaching on the kingdom of God, he did not want other people to know what he was teaching. So he quoted Isaiah to underline the fact that people would see without truly seeing; they would hear and not understand (Matthew 13:10–17).

Working in evangelism among Muslims, I could see the importance of what Jesus taught. Many of the people I related to day by day would have reacted violently if they had understood what I wanted to teach about Jesus. On one occasion I had been surrounded by a crowd of young Muslims armed with stones. Fortunately I escaped with only a mass of bruises. But this experience showed me the danger of casting our pearls before swine or giving dogs what is sacred (Matthew 7:6). Jesus warns that such people will not only 'tear you to pieces', but also trample the sacred pearls underfoot. In those days Malay Muslims were firmly opposed to the Christian faith. If I had witnessed openly with a clear message about Jesus, they would have reacted violently. I had already experienced that painfully in Singapore. Just telling stories seemed wiser!

In more recent years some Malays have become disillusioned with Islam and are more open to the gospel. Now
we have to be more discerning. When is it right to use parables
and when should we proclaim the good news of Jesus clearly
and openly?

By teaching in parables to people who are firmly against
the Christian message, therefore, there are three things which
are important to remember. Firstly, people may enjoy our
stories and come again for more some other time. We may
pray that they may then be more open spiritually. Secondly,
the name of the Lord and the glory of the gospel will not
be blasphemed and abused. Thirdly, rejecting Jesus and his
gospel is a hardening experience. In our love for people, we
don't want to cause their hearts to be hardened and thus make
it more difficult for them to trust the Lord in the future.
Although we long to present the fullness of the gospel to all
people without compromise, in practice we may meet people
who are in no way ready to receive it. If we present the gospel
to them in such a way that they are forced to make a definite
decision, they can only reject it. Rejecting Jesus inevitably
hardens the heart and makes it more difficult for people to
accept Christ later. In fact it may actually prove unloving
to press such people too hard and too quickly. We should ask
the Lord to give us the discernment to know when he wants
us to preach the gospel clearly and when it is right to teach
through parables.

In Britain too we may be faced with people who are rigidly
opposed to the Christian faith and in no way ready to accept
a direct witness to the gospel of Jesus. With such people it
may be wiser not to speak too clearly about the Lord. A
parabolic form of communication may prove more suitable.
We might even take over the parable of the widow's offering
and fit it into a Western context with two individuals giving

to Children in Need or some other charity. In Britain too the
question of our motives is highly relevant, but rarely discussed
openly. What motives move us in our charitable giving? We
may also enjoy inventing our own stories in parable form and
with a Western context.

Two men prayed

This parable became one of my favourites. As with the story
of the widow's offering, I related this parable too to the Muslim
teaching on *niyyah* (intention). But this time it was not centred
on paying one's *zakat* (alms), but on prayer. Prayer is of course
central in every faith, so a parable about prayer can be adapted
and used in any context in Britain or in any other country.

The local government hospital was open for visiting. 'Did
you hear about Haji Ahmed?' would again be my opening
gambit as I chatted with a couple of the patients. Other
patients and visitors would quickly gather round to learn the
gossip. A little entertainment could relieve the boredom of
long days in hospital.

Haji Ahmed was the leader of the whole Muslim
community in his town and led the mosque prayers five times
every day. On one particular Friday he made his way happily
to the mosque, going straight to the front of all the men as
they gathered. He made sure that the lines of men were
straight with no gaps between them. As every Malay Muslim
knows, an evil spirit will fill any gap between people as they
pray. Christians need to learn this if they live in a Muslim
country or society. In churches too we must not have gaps
between Christians, for it is not only a sign of lack of love,
but to our Muslim friends it shows that we have evil spirits
in our congregation!

Haji Ahmed's prayers were perfect. When performing the washings before prayer, he knew without hesitation the right way of washing the various parts of the body and he did so in just the right order. Much fun can be had in telling of this, for every Muslim knows the details of the washings. So one can 'forget' or pretend ignorance. The listeners will love to call out with all the satisfaction of knowing the right answers.

In the prayers the haji's ritual movements were perfect, in prostration his back was absolutely straight without any sign of a curve, his fingers were exactly parallel and in the direction of Mecca, his Arabic was beautifully correct in its pronunciation and in relation to his bodily movements. Perfect in every way!

But he was of course well able to perform his prayers without having to think carefully. Unfortunately that day his mind wandered to the young woman at the end of his street. She was beautiful, and the haji began to daydream of her. He would have loved to be like King David watching the naked Bathsheba having her bath.

Of course it is wrong mentally to undress an attractive person when one is doing one's prayers. But all Muslims would be keenly aware that all of us are weak and made of clay. God knows our weakness and he is very merciful. Allah would also see that Haji Ahmed's prayers were superbly in tune with his revealed will concerning the prayers. So surely Allah will be merciful towards the haji?

Now it happened that a couple of hours later a poor beggar was walking along the street past the mosque. This beggar had not been a good Muslim. He had not prayed since he was a boy with his grandmother; he had not fasted or paid any alms. And of course he had never even considered the possibility of performing the Hajj. But he was deeply conscious of God's goodness to him. He had always just about had enough to eat.

His clothes were far from smart, but they always covered his body adequately.

So the old beggar decided to go into the mosque to thank God. He went directly to the washing room, but could not remember how one does the ritual washings. He waited for a while, hoping that someone else would come and he could follow their example. But it was not one of the five prayer times and no-one came. Finally he just put his hands into the running water and washed his face and hands. He rubbed the back of his neck with water too to send a cool refreshing shiver down his spine.

Then he went into the mosque, leaving his slippers at the entrance. Feeling very inadequate and out of place, he went behind one of the great pillars and squatted cross-legged on the carpet. Again, he could not remember the prayers. His Arabic language had never been very wonderful, but now after so many years he could not recall a single word of it. And he couldn't recall the ritual movements. Finally he just began to pray in his own words in his native Malay language.

'God, I have not been a good Muslim. I have not prayed, fasted, performed the Hajj or paid zakat. But you have been so merciful to me and so kind. Please forgive me and help me to follow you and be obedient to your will.'

As with the story of the haji paying his zakat, I again asked people which man's prayers God considered better. The unspiritual young men would always fail to think seriously about my story. Their minds were filled with arguing about which young woman in their town was really beautiful. Conservative Muslims were convinced that God preferred the haji's prayers because they were in accordance with the revealed will of God. Of course they felt that he should not have been mentally undressing a woman while praying, but we are made of clay and God knows our weaknesses. God will surely be merciful.

Some people would realize that my story was trying to convey something deeper. Then I could just introduce the ideas of niyyah and ask whether God is more interested in the outward forms of prayer or in our heart motive when we pray.

In just a few lives, we saw the Holy Spirit awakening a real sense of repentance and desire for forgiveness and new life. We encouraged them to turn away from wrong motives in their religious practice. Forgiveness and new life through the death and resurrection of Jesus are the answer to their needs.

In Britain, or anywhere else, we can find people falling into the same danger of practising their faith through mere habit. It is so easy to overemphasize the outward forms of prayer and worship. In God's eyes the most important thing is the motive of our hearts in relationship with him. This issue dogs every society everywhere, so I find that these parables of the widow's offering (Mark 12:41–44; Luke 21:1–4) and of the two men praying (Luke 18:9–14) relate significantly in any context. Britain is certainly no exception. Of course a few details will need to be changed to fit the religion and culture.

'Cinderella'

Almost every society in every continent has traditional parabolic stories which are well known and loved. For example, in the English-speaking world the story of Cinderella is a favourite which everyone knows. Sometimes it is so much part of the tradition that people do not think about the lessons it conveys.

Cinderella lacks any power in this world and suffers the oppressive abuse of the older ugly sisters. How reminiscent

this is of the people of Israel under slavery in Egypt or in exile
in Babylon! It remains highly relevant to modern situations
of oppression, people trafficking and slavery. Many ordinary
workers in business or industry, secretaries or medical workers
also feel oppressed by bullying superiors. Violent domestic
abuse also oppresses many women and young people up and
down our land. But as the story unfolds, audiences look
forward with assured anticipation to the time when the ugly
sisters will be put to shame and lose their power over
Cinderella. God's judgment both of the Egyptians and the
Babylonians would surely come. And that remains true of all
oppressive powers. God's judgment will be evident and his
righteousness will be vindicated. In one way or another he
longs to deliver people from every form of oppression. This
is God's message to Habakkuk. The sin of Judah seems to
reign supreme. Then the victorious power of the horren-
dously rapacious and idolatrous Babylonians appears to have
gained unrivalled supremacy. But Habakkuk chapter 2 reveals
to us the reality of God's final judgment and the vindication
of God's faithful followers.[7] How encouraging for us too in
Britain today!

Cinderella herself will not only enjoy the actual dance until
midnight comes, but she will also become the much-loved
wife of the prince himself. As God's people it is heart-
warming that we can have times in which we enjoy the
luxuries and pleasures of life. But in those times of ease we
are always aware that midnight may strike at any moment
and we may have to return to the hard labour of Cinderella
under the oversight of the ugly sisters. Finally, however, we
know that the heavenly Prince will come to claim us as his
bride and we shall live eternally in the glorious splendour of
his unending love. God's ultimate gift of salvation is available
for us all.

Isaiah's words, quoted by Jesus, relate very obviously to English-speaking audiences as they enjoy the parabolic pantomime of Cinderella. Those with ears to hear may indeed rejoice in God's deliverance of the oppressed and the glory of our intimate relationship with the Prince, the very Son of God. We also look forward to the day when all oppressors will face the judgment of God, so that the justice and righteousness of our God may be seen by all people everywhere. But we realize too that most people just enjoy the pretty story of Cinderella without being aware that it is indeed a parable with a message. They see, but don't really see. They hear with their ears, but they don't really understand.

Enigmatic parables

We have already noted how Jesus used parables in his teaching so that those with ears to hear should indeed understand, but also to conceal the truth from those who were not open to receive him or his teaching.

Parables can therefore sometimes be enigmatic and debatable. For example, Jesus told a story to teach people how to pray (Luke 11:5–8). In his story a man had an unexpected visitor late at night. Unfortunately he had run out of bread and had nothing to put before his visitor. Very embarrassing in a society where hospitality was a fundamental virtue!

Quickly he ran next door to ask his neighbour for some bread to give to his visitor. But the neighbour and his family were already asleep. In many village societies around the world, family members just lie on the floor wherever they happen to fall asleep. In the midnight darkness with no electricity it is hard to avoid stepping on one of the sprawling bodies on the floor. So a neighbour may pretend not to hear the request for bread. How pertinent even today in many parts of the world are the neighbour's words, 'Don't bother me . . . I can't get up and give you anything' (Luke 11:7)! Even in New Testament times, without electricity it was not easy to crawl out of bed without disturbing the family.

The man will not get up just for friendship's sake, but finally he does give his neighbour the bread he is asking for because of his 'boldness'. The word really signifies 'shamelessness'. Did the neighbour finally get up and give the bread because he did not want to lose face? To refuse his friend's request would bring shame on both of them – the one because he refused to help, the other because he would fail to put food before his visitor. Or was Jesus thinking of the man's lack of shame in disturbing his neighbour at such an hour? The earlier New International Version (1984) translates 11:8 as 'because of the man's boldness' with the footnote 'or *persistence*', whereas the 2011 revision has the words 'shameless audacity'. The old King James Version uses the word 'importunity'. Perhaps we may say that the neighbour got up and gave the bread because the man made such a beastly nuisance of himself. He knocked and knocked, called and called, asked and asked.

Jesus applies this story with the well-known teaching: 'Ask and it will be given to you; seek and you will find; knock and the door will be opened to you' (Luke 11:9). The original Greek uses the continuous present tense. Ask and go on asking; seek and go on seeking; knock and go on knocking. God calls us to persist in prayer day in and day out, month in and month out, year in and year out.

Jesus' parable can be interpreted and applied in different ways. As with the other parables which we have outlined in this chapter, we have two options in telling the story. We can just tell the parable and leave the audience to apply it in whatever ways may fit their particular situation. Or we can do the work for our audience and draw a moral ourselves. Generally it may be better to accept the enigmatic nature of the parable and leave people to wrestle on their own with its meaning. I find it is often helpful just to suggest a few pertinent questions, so that people can more easily make a start in finding how the parable may speak to them with their particular background. British people love to struggle on their own with the meaning and significance of stories. They prefer to think things through for themselves rather than having the moral given to them on a plate. In this way too they are more likely to apply our parables in ways which relate more relevantly to their own situation.

Questions:

- What other stories besides 'Cinderella' are well known in Britain because of pantomimes? What hidden significance can you observe in their stories?
- Try retelling these stories in your own words with pertinent questions at the end to stimulate deeper thought.

8. DIFFERENT CULTURES TELL STORIES IN DIFFERENT WAYS

Hundreds of keen young South Korean Christians listened eagerly to our teaching on cross-cultural communication. When I mentioned that storytelling can be particularly relevant and effective as a form of teaching, a smile of appreciation spread immediately. Noting their obvious interest, I asked them whether this was also popular in South Korea. Nods of approval encouraged me further. Naughtily playing to the gallery, knowing their love for Jews and anything Jewish, I offered to tell them a couple of Jewish stories. Enthusiasm rippled through the hall.

I began with the well-known story of two Jewish farmers who were quarrelling over which of them owned one particular cow. They fought, each trying to drag the cow onto his own property. One took hold of the cow's horns and pulled the cow towards his field. The other farmer immediately grabbed the poor cow's tail and with all his might attempted to bring her in the opposite direction towards his cowshed.

Both pulled and pulled and pulled. Sometimes the one farmer seemed to gain the upper hand, while at other times the second farmer succeeded in moving the cow a few yards in his direction. Back and forth they struggled. Then a burly Roman soldier came and milked the cow!

My Korean students stared in uncertain amazement. Was the story already finished?

I have told this story not only in that Korean context, but also many times in Britain. The audience always enjoys the humour of the story with its picture of those two farmers pulling the cow in such a ridiculous manner. But they are shocked at the abrupt and totally unexpected ending, still wondering which of the two farmers actually won the day and got possession of the cow. They laugh at the thought of someone else actually enjoying the cow's milk, but generally don't grasp the wider significance of the story until I apply it for them.

In teaching the real meaning of this story, in Britain it may be suggested that an Anglican vicar and a Pentecostal minister were debating fiercely, while an imam came and converted their members to Islam! Are we quarrelling among ourselves while others gain the fruit which we should have gained together? This is a story which can be applied in all sorts of different contexts where disunity reigns. It is a simple, amusing story which anyone can tell.

This incident in South Korea led to fascinating discussions with some of their leaders. Why did their people not grasp the underlying meaning of that Jewish story? Why were the young people so shocked at the sudden conclusion? When telling the story in Britain, as a Jew myself I am sometimes surprised at my listeners' reaction to the typically Jewish twist at the end of the story. After all, the popular crime stories like Agatha Christie's generally end with some unexpected revelation which solves the crime and exposes the criminal. But most English stories do not have such short, sharp endings. Even Agatha Christie leaves her British readers with some degree of incredulity and uncertainty. How did Hercule Poirot perceive the clues which unravelled the whole situation with its complex relationships? We are left amazed and perplexed! But we love the stories and their dénouement, so it is evident that these unexpected conclusions do not spoil our enjoyment. In fact, these old crime stories continue to be read and watched on television from generation to generation. If we want, however, we can easily soften the suddenness of the Jewish end to the story and draw out the story's meaning with its relevant application.

Undeterred by the Korean students' bafflement, I unwisely ventured a second Jewish story. They encouraged me, hoping that this time they would feel more at home with my story.

Shortly after the time of Jesus, a great Jewish rabbi walked the streets of Jerusalem. Rabbi Akiva (AD 50–135) was widely known for his great learning, contributing significantly to the development of Judaism in the crucial years after the destruction of Jerusalem in AD 70. Jews came from near and far to consult with him and to profit from his wisdom.

One day a group of village elders came to the holy rabbi to seek his help. In their village near Jerusalem, poisonous snakes were biting people with fatal consequences. 'How can we rid our village of this scourge?' they asked the rabbi. Would he be willing to come out to their village and help them? Much to their relief the great teacher agreed to come.

On arrival in the village, Rabbi Akiva asked where they thought the poisonous snakes were coming from. The villagers pointed to a hole in the ground. The rabbi quickly

took off his sandals and thrust his bare heel into the hole, so
that the snakes could no longer get out. After a while one of
the poisonous snakes found its exit blocked and bit the rabbi's
heel – and the snake died!

Again the Korean young people did not appreciate that the
story had ended! And again, when I have told this story in
Britain and America, I find that people are always shocked at
the sudden ending and do not always grasp its significance. I
had to learn that the Jewish way of telling stories differs
radically from that of other nations. Every culture has its own
pattern of communication and tells stories in slightly different
ways. But such Jewish stories can also be adapted for a British
or Korean audience by softening the final conclusion to the
story and adding its meaning.

In explanation I like to ask the question, 'Who is greater,
the one who is in you or the one who is in the world?' (see
1 John 4:4). Which is greater, a poisonous snake or a holy
rabbi? So if a poisonous snake bites the rabbi, which one dies?!
The apostle Paul experienced this when he was shipwrecked
on Malta (Acts 28:3–6). A viper fastened itself to his hand, and
the islanders assumed that he would 'swell up or . . . fall dead'.
But Paul 'suffered no ill effects', so the people of Malta 'said
he was a god'.

What a reassuring message for Christians facing difficulties!
Young people at school may come up against bigger boys or
girls who delight to make life difficult for those weaker than
themselves. At work or in the office, Christians may experience bullying supervisors or managers. Increasingly, Western
Christians may have to suffer because of our moral convictions or in relation to abortion or same-sex marriage. And
in some other countries Christians may feel quite powerless in contexts of violent persecution. In such situations it is
enormously encouraging to be reminded that a poisonous

snake will die if it bites a holy rabbi and will not be able to hurt a man of God like Paul. Even if we do suffer in this world, ultimately the people of God will be vindicated and will experience the glory of God. God's victorious grace will finally always win against human sin.

Seeing that the Korean students did not appreciate the unexpected ending to the two Jewish stories and failed to grasp their significance, I began to enquire about their traditional Korean stories. What form do they come in? Local Christian leaders explained to me that their stories last longer and the conclusion usually conveys some moral teaching. Listeners generally foresee the final moral long before the story comes to an end. They enjoy the achievement of having worked out the point of the story before it was fully revealed. The feeling of 'I know what's coming' adds to the pleasure of listening. With this long drawn-out pattern of telling stories, the moral is clearly taught and understood.

Jewish listeners to Korean traditional stories are likely to find them somewhat tedious. They may not be willing to wait so long for teaching which they have long since anticipated. On the other hand, as we have seen, Koreans may not appreciate Jewish stories which can fail to convey their teaching adequately. I had to learn that telling Jewish stories in South Korea may not be a suitable way to communicate Christian truth. Likewise, Korean stories might not be appropriate in Tel Aviv. Cultural adaptation becomes essential in every cross-cultural context. So in Britain too we shall have to alter their stories to fit our context. Jewish stories may need to be somewhat lengthened and given less abrupt endings. Korean stories may need to be shortened and their conclusion made a little less obvious. But the basics of these stories may well be useful in every culture. With just a little adaptation, for example, these two Jewish stories will have much to teach in a British context. And happily they are easy to learn and teach – and in a fun-loving British culture they are both amusing.

Korean history has been intertwined with that of Japan for many centuries. For some years Korea was even under the expansionist power of Japan. So some people assume that Korean culture must relate closely to Japanese, but actually this is far from the case. Koreans often feel a deep antipathy towards the Japanese, while many Japanese look down on Koreans as inferior. This barrier between the two nations is further fuelled by their very different patterns of decision-making. It relates also to wider differences in communication, including the way they tell stories.

Traditional Japanese stories reflect the fact that the Japanese think of themselves as a suffering people. As a result, they developed a form of telling stories which commonly ended in tragic suffering. Wives die to protect the honour of their husbands or the lives of their children. Samurai warriors commit suicide to preserve their honour or to give honour to their prince. We are reminded of the words of Jesus to the city of Jerusalem: 'How often I have longed to gather your children together, as a hen gathers her chicks under her wings' (Matthew 23:37). We have become accustomed to the picture of a mother hen burning to death while her chicks remain in safety under her wings.

Japanese traditional stories form an easy bridge into the good news of Jesus' life and tragic suffering on the cross for our salvation. As Christians, however, we shall want to emphasize the glorious purpose of the suffering which is not usually stressed in the Japanese stories. We may feel somewhat critical therefore of the key Japanese theologian K. Kitamori (1916–98) in his book *The Theology of the Pain of God*.[8] He develops a similar emphasis on God's noble suffering on the cross of Jesus, but in his thinking the cross does not lead on to the life-giving resurrection. Just as traditional Japanese stories may end with the noble act of suffering for the honour or welfare of someone else, without any ensuing glory or rejoicing, so too Kitamori concentrates on the suffering of Jesus without progressing to the joy of Jesus' resurrection and ascension. As Christians in non-Japanese countries we shall need to add a resurrection conclusion to such Japanese stories. Suffering is never the end of our story, for the victory of God's grace is always the trump card. Stories which end with suffering, without leading on to new resurrection life, will fail to convey the full truth of the gospel even if they are following the pattern of traditional Japanese stories.

So I began to realize that cultural adaptation will have to include learning how to tell stories relevantly in another culture. In the globalized Britain of today we need to rethink our patterns of communication. We long for the gospel of Jesus to penetrate our neighbours' hearts and for the spiritual growth of young Christians of every cultural background. How then can we proclaim the gospel clearly, as we should (Colossians 4:3)?

People from ethnic minority backgrounds vary enormously. Some continue to live and think as if they were still living in the country of their family background. Others have adapted well into the surrounding culture and way of life. Many remain somewhere between those two positions, living in two cultures and not entirely at one with either of them. Some Koreans in Britain therefore no longer really appreciate traditional Korean stories, finding them dull. But others still feel at home with everything that is traditionally Korean. Likewise some British Jews will not understand traditional Jewish stories, for they have assimilated consciously or unconsciously into British cultural forms of communication. Ethnic British people from different generations and cultural backgrounds will also vary in their appreciation of traditional British stories. Nevertheless, we shall find that people of every background still appreciate communication by means of lively stories. In our multi-cultural society they have learned to a considerable degree to relate to a wide variety of ways of communicating. So keep telling stories!

Many British churches are now multi-ethnic. It is also true that the culture of one part of Britain may differ considerably from another part of the country – dour Yorkshire culture and communication patterns may not relate well in Celtic Cornwall, and vice versa! The generation gap has widened markedly in Western cultures, as indeed also in most other parts of the world. The more traditional forms of telling stories may prove effective for teaching Christian truth to the elderly, but youth have been deeply influenced by the more cryptic style of modern technology. They therefore need more cryptic, foreshortened stories. It is interesting that Jesus' parables fit both the elderly and younger people. Some of his parables are longer and include clear explanations of their meaning (e.g. the parable of the sower), while others are short and snappy (e.g. the parables of the hidden treasure and the pearl of great value – Matthew 13:44–46).

In the days of communism before the fall of the Berlin Wall in 1989, life for ordinary people in East European countries and Russia was terribly hard. The authorities did not permit any criticism, and the multitude of secret informers made it dangerous to voice any such negative thoughts outside one's bedroom. In our 'blame culture' with its love of criticism and complaint, British people would have found such oppression particularly difficult. Russians and East Europeans relieved their frustration by telling rather bitter, humorous stories.

British people, and other West Europeans, seem to enjoy these East European and Russian stories with their mixture of humour and critical discontent.

For example, Russians used to enjoy the story of a man who saved his money in order to buy a new car. Finally he had enough and went to the car salesroom. 'May I order a car, please,' he asked the salesperson. He made it clear what sort of car he wanted, paid the money, and the order was accepted.

'I am afraid your car will not be available for five years,' the salesperson informed the purchaser.

'That's fine,' he replied. 'Today is 1 September 1980, so it should be here on 1 September 1985. Is that right?'

'Yes,' came back the assurance. 'On 1 September 1985 your car will be here for you.'

'Will it be ready for me in the morning or the afternoon?'

'Does it matter? It's still five years from now.'

'Well, the plumber is coming in the morning that day.'

Reliable and prompt service was then a rare treat in the communist world. Serious trouble could fall on you if you complained about the lack of service. But people could work out their frustration through humorous stories which reflected the actual situations. We can all laugh at the thought of having to wait five years for the plumber to come, but it is desperately serious if one has to live in such circumstances. This story will be appreciated wherever people are facing inefficiency or bureaucratic delays. How often things are promised for a certain date, but fail to arrive! How often builders promise to do a job before a particular time, but their promise is not fulfilled! The Russian story will prove apt and we can go on to talk of God's absolute reliability and faithfulness in contrast. Or we can say how God makes promises, but does not give the date by which they will come to pass. But in his faithfulness God will always in his own good time keep his promises. Again, we may note that this Russian story is very simple and easy for anyone to recount and then apply.

Another such Russian story told of a little old woman going to the butcher's shop to buy meat. She took her place at the back of the long queue, but soon noticed that it did not progress forward. She then looked up and quickly saw that, as usual, there was no meat at all on the shop shelves. Hopefully at some stage some meat would be delivered and the people might be able to buy some for their families. Gradually, as time passed, one person after another abandoned hope and left the queue. Finally the elderly housewife alone remained and faced the two salespeople.

'Do you have any sausages?' she asked.

'No, you can see there are no sausages in the shop.'

'What about some chicken?'

The question met with the same reply.

'What about some pork?' was followed by 'What about some beef?' and 'What about some lamb?'

Each request met the same negative response.

Finally the old lady shrugged her shoulders and walked out of the shop.

'Why did that woman ask all those stupid questions?' the one salesperson asked the other. 'Surely she could see that we don't have anything on our shop shelves.'

'She was just showing off her good memory,' came the reply.

As with the previous story, one laughs at the stupidity of the old housewife and her whole situation. Listeners share in the humour of the final comment about the woman showing off her memory of better times. But the story also lets off the steam of frustration when all the shops have nothing but empty shelves. In such contexts even humorous stories can have a serious purpose. In Britain too many of us laughed at the humour of the television series *Yes, Prime Minister*, but in fact the humour reflected situations and characters which highlighted the commonly felt disillusionment with politics and politicians.

How wonderful it would be if we could develop Christian 'soaps' for television which subtly conveyed the message of the gospel in relation to people's actual feelings about our society! Likewise, humorous stories with a background of corruption, broken relationships and sin might introduce the gospel of holiness, love and hope. The British Christian drama group, Riding Lights, has given us a model for this. Some of their stories could easily be adopted in our local church or home group and acted out quite simply. Riding Lights stories really relate and can speak into the hearts of our people.

In Latin America, liberation theology[9] writers have developed cartoon stories of fictional characters struggling against their authoritarian political structures and leaders. The heroes come from peasant or slum backgrounds, so they understand the desperate need to bring social justice to their societies. The hunger for justice in society moves them to courageous exploits and to suffering for their cause. Christians in Britain today feel deeply the social problems of our world – human trafficking, political oppression, street kids and poverty, ecological and environmental concerns. So many social problems move our hearts. Perhaps some of us with artistic gifts could draw a series of cartoons or pictures to exhibit in our church or local library. Such pictures could also be shown informally to little groups of friends in our home or wherever we meet people. As we show the pictures, it is helpful too to explain the issues being depicted and the challenge of these social issues.

Popular European stories

Most European countries have developed a tradition of well-known fables which are told and retold not only to children, but also among adults. They have become part and parcel of the background knowledge with which our people used to be brought up. Although many in the younger generations have missed out on these brilliant tales and therefore lack the moral lessons which accompany such fables, with the older generations we may assume knowledge of at least some of these stories. So they can be used effectively in sharing Christian teaching. Younger people may not know the stories, but they too will thoroughly enjoy them when they are introduced to them.

The art of writing and telling fables with some moral instruction seems to stem very largely from the Greek Aesop (620–564 BC). Aesop was just a common slave, but his brilliance as a storyteller has had a wide influence all over the world. He lived at the same time as Siddhartha Gautama, the Buddha. Clear evidence of the influence of Aesop's fables is to be found in the Jatakas, the stories of the Buddha's former incarnations. As we have already noted, children in the Buddhist world are brought up with these stories as the foundation of their religious faith. But their influence is particularly marked in Europe, leading to the rise of great writers of fables in various European countries. For example, in Russia Ivan Krylov (1769–1844) became famous for writing more than 200 fables. Some of his stories are taken directly from Aesop, but in his later years he thought up original tales which matched Aesop's for brilliance. Traditionally in Russia and other Slavonic cultures, Krylov's fables have formed an essential part of most children's home education. Throughout the seventy years of communism in Russia, the works of

Krylov were printed and distributed, so his fables are still well known there.

In Britain, Aesop's fables became hugely popular in the eighteenth century with several editions being published by a wide variety of writers. Together with these fables came considerable moral application and teaching in accordance with the Christian faith. In this way Aesop's fables became an integral part of British thought and influenced the whole moral conscience of the nation. In 1912 the well-known artist Arthur Rackham drew the illustrations for a major edition of Aesop's fables, so that still today some of the stories are well known. We can find everyday expressions in the English language which stem from this background. For example, Aesop has a short fable called 'The Boy Who Cried Wolf' (no. 210 in the Perry Index). Still today we continue to use the expression 'to cry wolf' without realizing where it originally came from.

In Aesop's original story a shepherd boy continually tells the local villagers that a wolf is attacking his flock. When eventually a wolf does attack the sheep and he calls to the villagers for help, they do not believe him and his flock is destroyed. In the original Greek version the moral observes that this 'is how liars are rewarded. Even if they tell the truth, no-one believes them.' In modern Britain truth has largely lost its moral value, so this old story regains a vital relevance for our society. Christians will want not only to stress the desperate need in our modern society for truth, but will also show how God himself is truth personified and his Word is totally true. We can trust everything God says in his Word. And God's truth is the inspiration which produces truth in his people.

Equally well known and relevant to our generation in Britain and the rest of Europe is Aesop's old tale, 'The Tortoise and the Hare' (no. 226 in the Perry Index). In this well-known fable a hare mocks the tortoise which moves so very slowly. The tortoise then challenges the nimble hare to a race. Unsurprisingly, at first the hare easily outruns the slow-moving tortoise. Being far ahead of the tortoise, the hare relaxes and takes a nap. Meanwhile the tortoise continues slowly, but steadily, to make progress. It is not easy for the tortoise and he becomes desperately exhausted, but still he doggedly perseveres and finally reaches the finishing line before the hare. So the slow tortoise wins, not the speedy hare.

Over the centuries various applications have been deduced from this fable. Some have pointed out that the hare's pride and overconfidence proved his downfall. The story is therefore teaching the supreme value of humility even when you suspect that you may be more gifted than those around you. This relates well to biblical teaching, in which humility and meekness form the precondition of almost every promise of God in the Bible. How important it is in the life of a church that we consider others better than ourselves (Philippians 2:3)! All over our country, people are leaving churches because their pastor does not match up to their expectations or because they feel critical of other church members. Pride can tempt us to ignore the plank in our own eye, while concentrating our criticism on the speck in our neighbour's (Matthew 7:3–5).

Knowing the Bible well, others point out that in Ecclesiastes 9:11 it is stated that 'the race is not to the swift or the battle to the strong'. In applying Aesop's fable, they underline the biblical teaching that God's election and call frequently come to the youngest in the family (e.g. King David) and to the weak (e.g. Gideon in Judges 6:15). Even the people of Israel were not chosen because they were a large or gifted people, for they 'were the fewest of all peoples' (Deuteronomy 7:7). Perhaps today God's grace and glory will come across more powerfully in Britain and other countries of Europe, for the churches now hold only a small minority of our populations. When the church is despised, ignored and evidently powerless in society, then God may use its witness most effectively.

Whichever application one chooses, the story of the tortoise and the hare retains its vital significance and relevance for our modern British context.

Perhaps it should be noted that actually Ecclesiastes 9:11 contains a different truth: 'Time and chance happen to them all' – the swift, strong, wise, brilliant and learned share the same fate as everyone else. When Ayatollah Khomeini gained power, a professor of science at Tehran University was interviewed by the BBC as he led an enthusiastic mass demonstration. Excitedly he declared his assurance that Allah would now bless Iran with fantastic prosperity. Because Iran would now follow Islamic law and Islam would rule in the nation, he declared triumphantly, Allah would surely cause it to rain when rain was needed and the sun to shine when the crops required sunshine. At the time, I thought of Jesus' teaching that God 'causes his sun to rise on the evil and the good, and sends rain on the righteous and the unrighteous' (Matthew 5:45). What has happened now to that professor's assurance of Allah's blessing of the people of Islam? The story of the tortoise and the hare with its application through Ecclesiastes 9:11 could speak tellingly into his false Islamic prosperity theology – as also into its parallels in some Christian churches.

The Greek philosopher Apollonius (AD 15–100) declared that 'Humble incidents teach great truths'. This saying certainly fits the teaching of Jesus just a few years earlier. Aesop's fables and those which follow him also use simple incidents and easy-to-understand stories to communicate great truths. In our cultural contexts today in modern Europe we shall do well to follow in the footsteps of Jesus and the fable-writers like Aesop. We don't have to be brilliantly clever or gifted to make the message of Jesus come alive to the people around us. We can use simple stories like those of Aesop or tell simple incidents in our everyday life to introduce the great truths of the gospel. Modern IT also makes this particularly easy, for we can look up the stories of Aesop and others on the net.

For the French-speaking world Jean de la Fontaine (1621–95) wields enormous influence; his stories and poems are widely known. His fables reveal that he was well read, drawing his inspiration not only from Aesop, but also from Indian and Persian sources. The Buddhist Jatakas also contain parallels to some of the fables which Lafontaine wrote centuries later. Thus, Lafontaine's 'The Wolf and the Lamb' relates closely to the Jatakas' story of the Panther and the Goat. Lafontaine may well have borrowed from the fifteenth-century Scottish poet Robert Henryson in his fable 'The Wolf and the Lamb'. Later even *Punch* magazine adapted this fable in a cartoon of the French army dressed as a wolf staring across the Mekong River at a small, innocent Thai lamb. British imperialism strongly opposed French expansionism! So we see that in the world of storytelling, globalization seems to have been evident a long time ago! The story of the wolf and the lamb appears in various forms worldwide in different guises. In Aesop's fables it appears as 'The Cock and the Cat'.

In Lafontaine's version a hungry wolf encounters a defenceless lamb and desires to eat it for its breakfast. The wolf justifies its greed by accusing the lamb of various misdemeanours, all of which are proved untrue by the lamb. But the wolf is unwilling to listen to the words of the lamb. Determined to satisfy its hunger despite the injustice of its exercise of power, the wolf gobbles up the lamb.

The moral most commonly deduced from the story is that tyrants will brook no excuses. They are determined to use their superior strength to satisfy their own hunger for power, material prosperity and position. Already before Lafontaine, the Scottish Henryson had argued that the greedy and unjust wolf represents three groups of oppressive powers – corrupt lawyers, greedy landowners and aristocrats who exploit their tenants. However much people may protest against such corruption and oppression, those with muscle continue in their evil ways. In some ways it seems that the world has changed very little! This fable by Lafontaine could fit ideally into our teaching on the need for social justice in our corrupt world. As Christians we are reminded too that Jesus won our salvation in weakness through the way of the cross, not through the exercise of his divine power. It is the meek who inherit the earth. Jesus laid aside his glory and 'did not consider equality with God something to be grasped' (Philippians 2:6). Paul goes on to state that it was because of Jesus' deliberate choice of the lowly path that God the Father highly exalted him. Through Jesus' crucifixion we gain salvation, and Jesus attains the resurrection and ascension to the right hand of the Father.

Lafontaine's fable 'The Lion and the Mouse' has also entered into many European cultures, not only in the French-speaking world. It has played a significant part in shaping moral values in Britain and other European countries.

In this fable a little mouse happens to wake a great lion from its sleep. The lion is angry and threatens to eat the mouse. But the mouse begs for forgiveness and points out that a mere mouse is hardly worthy prey for a mighty lion. The lion will gain no honour for having eaten a little mouse. The lion is persuaded and allows the mouse to escape unharmed. Later the lion is captured by hunters in a net.

Totally entangled in the hunters' net, the lion has no way of escape. But the little mouse comes, sees the lion's position and gnaws through the ropes of the net. In this way the mouse saves the lion.

The moral of the story is clear. If we show mercy to others, we shall ourselves in turn receive mercy. God himself acts on this principle – 'forgive us our sins, as we forgive the sins of those who sin against us.' Jesus taught this in the Sermon on the Mount: 'Blessed are the merciful, for they will be shown mercy' (Matthew 5:7). Mercy and forgiveness breed reciprocal mercy and forgiveness.

In later English versions of this fable, the mouse promises to return the lion's favour when the lion shows mercy to it. The lion is sceptical and cannot believe that a mere mouse could ever be in a position to show mercy to a great lion, the very king of all beasts. The English application is thus slightly different from the original Aesop and Lafontaine version. God can use weak and ordinary people to bring his mercy and salvation to the powerful and mighty. Very ordinary people can tell powerful stories! In Matthew 28 the Great Commission is given to disciples who were 'afraid' (Matthew 28:5, 9–10) and some of them 'doubted' (Matthew 28:17). God often uses weak Christians to achieve his great purposes of showing mercy to the world through the proclamation of his gospel.

In this book we can only touch on a few better-known fables, but in our teaching of Christian truth and morals these fables give us wonderful material. They can be used to great effect in our Sunday schools or Bible classes for people of all ages. With little groups of friends or acquaintances we can say, 'I have come across an amazing old fable; have you heard the one about . . . ?' and then launch into the telling of the story and its application. Their vivid and amusing style adds to the basic agenda of Bible stories.

In Britain we enjoy a rich vein of fables and traditional stories which are widely known throughout the country. Pantomimes have helped to disseminate some of these stories, so that children grow up with them. Some originate right back in the mists of time. For example, Sir Francis Palgrave may have said that the story of Jack and the beanstalk came to the shores of Britain with the Vikings, but some think it may even go back beyond the time of the Vikings.

On the other hand we have translated and adopted many stories from the German brothers, Jacob and Wilhelm Grimm (1785–1863 and 1786–1859) and the Danish Hans Christian Andersen (1805–75). Built on the foundation of the Grimm brothers and Hans Christian Andersen have come a variety of British writers of fables. Many of us have grown up with these enthralling stories. Our hearts echo the three bears' growling question, 'Who's been eating my porridge?' or the wolf's threat, 'I'll huff and I'll puff and I'll blow your house down.' Based on the Grimms' story of Little Red Riding Cap, the innocent little girl in her red hood has captured our imaginations. With the big bad wolf dressed in her grandmother's nightdress and pretending to be asleep in Grandmother's bed, little Red Riding Hood's dialogue with the wolf remains firmly in our memories throughout our lives:

'What a deep voice you have!' elicits the reply, 'All the better to greet you with.'

'What big eyes you have!' The wolf replies, 'All the better to see you with.'

'What big hands you have!' brings the threatening response, 'All the better to grab you with.'

And finally, 'What a big mouth you have!' with the reply, 'All the better to eat you with.'

Nevertheless little Red Riding Hood finally escapes the clutches of the big bad wolf. The evils of life seem so overwhelmingly threatening and powerful, but God finally will deliver his people. We can trust him both in this life and for eternity.

This story also warns us not be too naïve. Sin and evil may be dressed up to look innocuous and attractive, but the outward dress may still contain a wolf within.

Once again we may note that these popular stories can win hearts and minds without any clever presentation. It is so easy for us all to modulate our voice to sound like the wolf's growling threats and little Red Riding Hood's sweet girl's words.

Lewis Carroll (1832–98) with his *Alice in Wonderland* and Beatrix Potter (1866–1943) and *The Tale of Peter Rabbit* enthral us all. Likewise A. A. Milne's *Winnie-the-Pooh* and *Toad of Toad Hall*, with such characters as Badger, Ratty and Mole, live with us throughout our lives. It is good to think through these stories and see how they can be used to teach the glories of the Christian message.

In many cultures around the world some particular animal becomes the key character. There may well be a number of different stories which centre on that animal, and indeed all the characters of the stories may be animals. Thus in Indonesia and Malaysia people tell a variety of old stories about a clever little mousedeer, Sang Kancil, who outwits the larger and more powerful jungle animals. Such well-known animal stories can prove very effective if some Christian teaching is deduced from them. Many of the fables of Aesop, Lafontaine, the Grimm brothers, Hans Christian Andersen, Beatrix Potter and others are animal stories. In World War 2 the bulldog became a vital factor in strengthening British resolve. Throughout the generations, children easily imagine themselves to be the American Brer Rabbit or some other animal character. It may be good to convey Christian teaching partly through stories with animals as the characters. We may also be able to adopt traditional animal stories and adapt them to convey a Christian message.

How wonderful it would be if we could add a Christian element into these stories to promote good over evil, to show the victory of God through the resurrection of Jesus. The Grimm brothers themselves told various lesser-known stories which reflect their Christian background. For example, they told the story of twelve desperately poor brothers who are rocked to sleep magically by an angel boy. Their great longing was not just for bread to eat, but particularly to see the coming Saviour. After 300 years of sleep, God rewarded their heart's desire with a vision of Jesus who sent them out in apostolic mission.

In their well-known 'Hansel and Gretel' the Grimm brothers have the repeated refrain 'God will help' – and God does indeed help most wonderfully!

Hans Christian Andersen's fables lend themselves to being used for Christian teaching. For example, his 'The Emperor's New Suit' tells the story of a tailor deceiving the king into believing that he has an exceptionally fine new suit. In fact, the tailor has not produced anything at all, but persuades everyone that good intelligent people can see the new set of clothes whereas ordinary people are blind. Such people, the tailor says, cannot discern the king's new clothes. So the king goes everywhere half-naked, thinking that he has put on the new suit. He does not dare to say that he is neither good nor intelligent and therefore cannot see that he has no outer clothing on at all. All his courtiers also want to believe that they can see the king's magnificent new suit. Finally a small child tells the king that he has no suit on and the fraud is uncovered.

In our modern societies we need to teach that God will cause deceitful corruption to be exposed. The biblical word

'Be sure that your sin will find you out' (Numbers 32:23) comes as a much-needed warning to people of all ages and in every profession. It may be observed too that in this story it is a little child who finally informs the king of the tailor's deception. This fable reinforces the lesson from other stories that God often uses small and weak people as his instruments. It is often pointed out that it was just a young girl from Israel who encouraged the great army commander, the Syrian Naaman, to go to the prophet Elisha (not the king) for healing from his leprosy. His healing also came through washing himself in the despised little River Jordan. Naaman had to learn the humbling lesson that God often uses a little girl or boy and an insignificant river as his means of healing (2 Kings 5:1–14). How amazing that Jesus did not come to earth as a king, but as a carpenter's son in lowly Nazareth! And still today the Holy Spirit uses ordinary people in his service.

In Hans Christian Andersen's story 'The Princess and the Pea' (1835), the prince anxiously searched for a real princess. He met many princesses, but none of them seemed genuine. One night there was a knock at the palace door and outside stood a girl in the pouring rain. Her clothes looked fearfully bedraggled as she was wet through, but she claimed that she was a true princess. Could this half-drowned girl be a genuine princess?

To test her, the queen put a hard pea on her bed and covered it with twenty mattresses and twenty eiderdowns. In the morning the old queen asked the girl how she had slept. 'Badly,' she replied. 'I was lying on something hard and my body is black and blue all over.'

The queen reckoned that only a true princess could be so sensitive. So the prince and the princess married and lived happily ever after.

What a lesson for us in God's church! God earnestly desires true Christians, not just those who claim to be one. Jesus will only have true princesses as his bride. Many may claim to be a 'princess', but the Son of the King of kings will only be united with those who are genuine in their repentance and faith in Jesus as Messiah, Lord and Saviour. Outward appearances may deceive, but in Andersen's story the old queen discerns the genuine nature of the princess. She appeared bedraggled in the heavy rain and her clothes were far from regal in appearance, but she passed the old queen's test. The first letter of John gives us the various proofs which demonstrate whether we are truly children of God.

Perhaps we might apply the story to show that God can also make us to be sensitive, as true children of the King of kings. As we love one another, our sensitivity will not be physical, as in the story, but will be characterized by genuine empathy in our relationships with other people. As Christians we may pray for the spiritual gift of discernment, that we may sense people's real character and needs. What a gift for any pastoral or discipling ministry! It is also invaluable if our work includes interviewing applicants for a college course or job.

With a little imagination and thought, traditional fables and stories can become fascinating tools in communicating aspects of biblical truth and moral values. They can be widely used in evangelism, as also in church teaching to Christians of all ages and backgrounds. The continuing success of pantomimes year after year demonstrates the fundamental role such stories play in our society. As Christians we would do well to jump on this continually popular bandwagon.

Questions:

- Which children's fables or fairy stories were you brought up with as a child? What did you learn from them? How could you apply them now as a Christian and for adults?
- What proofs of being a genuine child of God can you discover in John's first letter? Work carefully through the letter. Then ask yourself how the above story of the princess and the pea can be used to give us this assurance.

CONCLUSION

'Grannie, can you tell us a story, please?' The children are tired after a long day paddling in the local river and enjoying a picnic. Cuddled up together on the sofa, they relax and all enjoy this experience of family love and oneness. Sometimes Grannie or Grandpa will find one of the old books which we used to read to the children's parents when they were young. Sometimes we tell them a story from our own experience in past years, or a traditional tale like 'Cinderella'. The grandchildren love it and join in with their own comments or memories from having heard the story before. What a delight both for the grandchildren and for the grandparents!

We rejoice in the thought that similar storytelling times are happening in many homes up and down our country. Bedtime too presents great opportunities for short stories with the children. When the children are tucked up comfortably and snugly in their beds, a Bible incident or some other story with a Christian input prepares the children wonderfully for happy and peaceful sleep. Parents, grandparents and other relatives of every background are still entrancing their children with beautiful stories in spite of the rival attractions of television and other media.

When I speak about telling stories and encourage Christians to try this method of communication, people often demur and begin to make excuses. They tell me that they don't think they have the gift of storytelling and feel sure that they could never become a storyteller. British Christians are particularly lacking in the necessary self-confidence. 'Do you sometimes tell your nephew or niece a story before they go to bed?' I ask them. When they confess that they have often done so, I comment that all of us from time to time tell stories to children or even to other adults. So there is no excuse to stop us using this pattern of teaching in order to share the good news of Jesus with other people.

Of course, some Christians will have a particular gift in this direction and will tell stories with special skill. Others will work hard to develop this gift and with increasing experience will learn to tell stories with interest, gusto and relevance. Yet others will stumble through the occasional story with some hesitation, but nevertheless children will lap up the stories they read or tell. This is true not only for storytelling, but for every form of communication – sharing one's personal testimony, gossiping the gospel with neighbour or friend, teaching the Bible in a home group or other Christian gathering. But with the help of God's Holy Spirit we can all play our part in all these different forms of Christian ministry, including telling stories.

A reminder – you can do it too!

Don't forget that telling a story well is in many ways rather similar to the art of acting in a play. When we were children, most of us had times when we pretended to be a prince or princess or even an animal. We can all tell a simple story. Just remember the following points. In your storytelling try to enter as far as possible into the character of the different personalities. It is good to engage with their feelings and desires. We want the characters to come alive to our audience. Stories should be told in a lively and expressive voice with plenty of emotion. We may like to change the timbre of our voice to reflect the situation. So we may lower our voice to heighten an atmosphere of danger or threat. A slight quaver can convey a dark or spooky mood. Sometimes we shall speak with a lively voice and with rather more volume, while at other times in the story it may be more appropriate to speak more slowly and softly. It is usually helpful to use some direct speech in our stories. Questions and exclamations add to the interest. Grunts and groans, animal noises and expressive sounds like 'Brrrr' for the cold contribute to making the story more arresting.

Our listeners will generally enjoy it if we make our own comments as we go along. Such comments may relate the story to something they themselves know and experience. Children will love it if we turn to them and make some comment like, 'Your teddy would be very frightened, wouldn't he, if he met a big bad wolf.' Or we may like to ask the child or children, 'What would your teddy feel if he met a big bad wolf like that?' If they are shy to answer, we may prompt them with 'Do you think he would run away? Or do you think he would be very brave and stand up to the big bad wolf?' We should remember that children's cuddly animals are to them not just an inanimate toy bought from a toy shop – their teddy is a living personality to them. For adults too, relevant comments or questions may be thrown in, such as 'We all know what it feels like to be short of cash!'

Adding drama

In telling stories it is good to remind ourselves of the little tricks which pantomimes use with phenomenal success year after year. Sometimes they have one word or short expression which they use again and again through the evening. They ask the children to shout it out whenever it comes up, pausing a moment as a sign that this word or expression is due. Such repetition goes over well in telling stories not only to children, but also to adults. In the Bible, repetition of a word is used to emphasize a thought, and in stories today such repetition of a word can also ensure that the moral of the story penetrates into people's minds. Adults too enjoy the feeling that they have something to add to our story, so they love to have a word or phrase which they can call out from time to time. There will always be a smile or laugh as they do so! For example, we noted this earlier in the Jungle Doctor story of the little snake. The father snake's repeated 'Be sure your sin will find you out!' is easy for people to learn off by heart and is ideal for everyone to call out repeatedly in suitable places in the story. Hopefully, afterwards they will remember this key sentence.

When I used to tell Islamicized forms of Jesus' parables among Muslims in Malaysia, I often made use of another weapon in the pantomime's armoury. Some pantomime characters are made out to be slightly stupid or ignorant, so they repeatedly forget something or are sadly ignorant of particular things which are well known to the audience. I would often include an older Muslim man who had not prayed since he was a boy with his grandmother. Now, after so many years, he couldn't remember how to do the ritual washings. He had forgotten the Arabic words in the prayers and the details of when and how to perform the prostrations and other set body

movements in prayer. I would pretend that I too did not know
these things. My audiences would gain great pleasure in
calling out instructions on such matters. Of course every
Muslim man there would know such everyday religious
matters and they loved to show their knowledge. In this way
people's attention was fixed on the story and they listened
carefully with great interest to everything that I said.

In Britain one might include in a story details of main
places of interest in London – Big Ben, Buckingham Palace,
Madame Tussaud's and others. A British audience would love
to prompt the storyteller if he/she makes it clear that he/she
has forgotten such names or indeed just doesn't know them.
In more Christian circles the storyteller might conveniently
'forget' how many Gospels there are and who wrote them.
Other very basic facts from the Bible or church life could also
be carefully 'forgotten'. In this way the listeners' attention is
riveted on the storyteller and what is being recounted. Little
'tricks of the trade' like this can help enormously in making
our stories more interesting to listen to. They are equally
helpful whether one is telling a story just to one child or to a
whole group of people. And all of us can easily learn them.

Stories can be used in informal conversation, in small
groups of children or adults, as indeed also in the context of
larger meetings. Telling one of my own stories, I have often
asked a person or a group of people whether they have heard
the story of . . . On rare occasions someone has quickly
replied that they do indeed know that particular story and
have heard it before. There is no need to feel embarrassed by
this answer! I continue by reminding them of some aspect of
the story and telling them what I particularly enjoy about it.
This can lead on to discussion of its application. But generally
I find that no-one knows the story or fable to which I have
referred. That allows me then to continue and actually tell

them the story. Home meetings are an ideal setting for telling a story with its application and meaning. As we saw earlier, the story of the peanut farmer and his pet dog or monkey fits wonderfully for a Christmas party or meeting.

On one occasion I used a story as my sermon in a village church. An older local man sat in splendid isolation in the choir stalls with his choir robes on. He was very proud of always knowing all the village gossip and scandal. 'Did anyone hear about Fred Baker?' I began. Immediately there came a confident reply from the choir stalls: 'Yes, I know Fred Baker.' Of course my 'Fred Baker' was a fictional character, but the old village man did not know that. I was then able to tell my story in dialogue with him – and I don't think he ever knew that 'Fred Baker' was fictional or that his pretending to know him was clear to me. But doing the story by dialogue helped make the story even more fascinating than it would have been otherwise. In any situation it may prove interesting if we can so manage things that our story is told in dialogue with one or more of our listeners.

As I learned when living and working in Malaysia, stories may prove to be the ideal form of communication in countries where the law forbids Christian witness or where hostility against the Christian faith makes straight witness too dangerous and unwise. Police spies frequently followed me and even tried to catch me out by asking questions about the Christian faith, hoping that I would then share the gospel with them and they could accuse me of proselytizing. But they could not object to me telling Islamicized biblical parables, such as I have described earlier, because I never said they were from the Bible and I didn't directly mention anything about Jesus. But my stories opened the door for the Holy Spirit to work in people's consciences and bring them to repentance and a strong desire for salvation and cleansing from their sin.

Such stories could be safely told even in the heart of Saudi Arabia with all the religious police surrounding the Christian!

In many British cities we now have whole areas which are largely Muslim. Open and direct Christian witness may prove quite unacceptable in such areas. Likewise in our aggressively pluralist society, Christian witness or even the slightest mention of the Christian faith may not be allowed in schools or other workplaces. But no-one can object to us telling a traditional fable or story in such a way that people are moved towards the Christian gospel and challenged that their secular lifestyle may not be fully satisfactory.

Churchill and preparation

'Before Winston Churchill spoke in parliament he carefully prepared his speech,' someone told me when I was just setting out on a ministry of speaking and preaching. 'He determined what vocabulary to use in each sentence. He then worked on his facial expressions, so that his argument was further underlined by what was written on his face. He even thought through and practised his gesticulations, so that every part of his speech came across with maximum effect. Finally, he thought through what questions or objections he was likely to face as a result of his speech, and then rehearsed his replies.' What a challenge for a young, inexperienced Christian speaker!

If Churchill could work so hard in preparation of his parliamentary speeches, should not I prepare even more thoroughly before speaking in the service of Jesus Christ? Why should we Christians be less professional than secular speakers? If a highly experienced politician like Churchill still felt the need for such detailed preparation, how dare I as a less experienced speaker remain ill-prepared and amateur in the service of the King of kings! Hearing that Churchill even delivered his talks in front of a mirror with a clock in front of him, I determined to do the same.

One day I was alone at home in my mother's house, so I delivered my sermon for the coming Sunday with all the facial expressions and gesticulations I had determined on. Little did I know that the man who helped my mother with her garden was stone deaf. I failed to see that he was standing just outside the window of the room where I was. He heard nothing, but saw me gesticulating energetically and thought I was somehow rebuking him! I learned to be more careful where and when I did my preparation!

My friend's words about Churchill reminded me of my childhood. When I was a small boy aged eight or nine, my French teacher called me to him after class one day. As a rather shy little boy, I was amazed when he said to me, 'When you grow up, I think you will become a public speaker. If you like, you can come to me after classes sometimes and I will teach you how to deliver a good talk.' As far as I know, this teacher was not a committed Christian, so I still wonder where his insight came from. He quietly taught me how to use my voice, how to show the right emotions in my facial expressions and in the use of my hands in my gesticulations, how to use pauses helpfully for effect, and other details of good communication in public speaking. If you are serious about communicating through stories, try to find someone who can guide you and help you to grow in this art.

If we are going to use stories publicly, proper preparation and practice will help enormously. Likewise, if we want to tell the same story several times in personal conversation, in children's bedtime stories or in other situations, careful preparation will pay handsome dividends. When I first began to tell stories in Thailand, I found it best just to work on two stories. Concentrating on just two stories allowed me to develop expressive vocabulary and to think through possible repartee which might develop with the people listening. Of course after a while I got to know these two stories extremely well and therefore felt much freer in my use of them. I had only been in Asia for just over a year, so inevitably my language was somewhat limited and that forced me to limit myself to just those two stories. I would recommend this to all who are setting out on storytelling. It is helpful to start with just two stories even in one's own language. Afterwards one can widen that repertoire.

Leave them hanging or give the application?

My experience of telling stories started in Muslim contexts. In most situations Muslims need time to think through their need of the gospel, the truths of the Christian message, what it would mean if they became Christians and whether they are willing to pay the cost of following Jesus as Lord and Saviour. It therefore seemed wise to allow the challenges of my stories to hang in the air without demanding any immediate response. In the weeks and months after telling a story, it was my prayer that the Holy Spirit would work in people's hearts, minds and wills to bring them to repentance and faith in Jesus the Messiah. What an encouragement it was when one or another would come to me, sometimes months after hearing a story, and say, 'I can't get that story out of my mind. My religious motives are selfish and wrong. How can I get right motives in relation to God?' Generally, such people would not use biblical vocabulary with words like 'repentance', 'faith' or 'salvation'. But this is what they really meant.

In Asian Muslim contexts I found that people commonly used pictorial language and stories in ordinary conversation, so they often had little difficulty in discerning the underlying significance of stories and enjoyed working that out for themselves. They could then apply it in their own way, even though I left the stories hanging at the end.

But in British, American and other Western contexts I find that people are not generally accustomed to understanding the teaching that underlies a story. They may need some help in gaining insight into its message. This can be done by some leading questions at the end of our narrative. One can also suggest what teaching and challenge is being presented. They may not appreciate too direct an application. But as we have already seen, a one-sentence challenge, repeated again and again throughout the story, can underline your main point. I have often used this approach with the Jungle Doctor stories.

Which methodology?

As we reach the end of this book on telling stories, it is important to stress that no methodology has all the answers. No way of communicating can guarantee success in bringing the good news of Jesus Christ effectively, either in evangelism or in teaching and discipling believers. In his sovereign grace, God can use any method to penetrate our hearts and minds with his gospel. Equally, everyone's free will makes it only too possible for them to reject or misunderstand God's Word. Fables and stories represent an excellent communication method, and people tend to remember stories even years after they hear them. Nevertheless, it has to be said that our stories will not automatically produce spiritual fruit.

Storytelling and love

In telling stories, as in all Christian communication, it is vitally important that we love the people we speak to. Even when we are holding forth to a larger congregation or crowd, we shall want to do everything possible to form a relationship with them. This can be done by making sure that we do not hesitate to look our audience in the face and from time to time catch the eye of people in the various sections of the crowd. Our facial expressions also should demonstrate a personal touch so that we do not seem too separated from our listeners or too aloof. If people feel that we relate to them and that we are characterized by genuine love, our stories and their teaching will carry much more weight.

For us as Christians, telling stories is not just a fun activity. And our aim is not just to entertain, although we very much hope people will enjoy our storytelling. Even less should we just be looking for our own popularity, although if we tell our stories well people will like us and think highly of us. But our goal should always remain the praise and honour of the Lord. To him be all glory now and for ever!

Storytelling and prayer

In communicating Christian truth it is vitally important that the Word should be accompanied by prayer. So in Colossians 4:2–6 the apostle Paul has his teaching on prayer in juxta-position with God opening a door for our message and with proclaiming the gospel clearly. In answer to our prayer, God can move in people's hearts and minds to make them open to his Word. It is always God, not our communication skill, who so works that people and indeed whole societies or strata of society can become responsive to the message of Christ. We therefore should be praying that the seed of our stories will fall on good, fertile ground and produce a rich harvest for God's glory.

In Colossians 4 Paul gives us three fundamental pillars of prayer. Firstly, we are to 'devote' ourselves to prayer. He urges us to persevere in prayer day after day, year after year and even decade after decade. The second pillar of prayer warns us that we need to be 'watchful'. This word takes us back to the story of Jesus' disciples in Gethsemane. Jesus called them to pray with him in his time of desperate need, but they slept. They were exhausted and needed sleep, so Jesus calls them not just to pray, but to 'watch and pray'. In our busy lives with the pressure of so many things on our minds and the telephone ringing, we also need to 'watch' in prayer. We can easily get distracted. Paul's third injunction is to be thankful in our prayers. We are called to rejoice in all the Lord is and does in our lives.

As we follow these three elements in prayer, our story-telling can gain spiritual life and bear much fruit.

Storytelling and the Holy Spirit

In the New Testament, Word and Spirit walk hand in hand together. We are weak, and Jesus reminds us that apart from him we can do nothing (John 15:5). However brilliant and well trained we may be, it still remains true that genuine spiritual fruit can only come from the hand of God. On our own, without the power of God's Spirit, our Christian life and our witness can only lead to frustration and despair. Our words (even through stories) without the life-giving work of the Holy Spirit will prove to be dead and will not bring resurrection life to our audiences. But likewise, spiritual fervour without the truth of the Word remains mere hot air and froth. It is the Word and the Spirit together which combine to bring the power of God into operation. Together they will change people's lives, renewing their spirits with the saving work of Jesus. It is noteworthy that in Acts 1:8 the power of the Spirit is inseparably linked to becoming Jesus' witnesses both in the disciples' home area of Jerusalem and Judea, and also in the wider world of Samaria and the 'ends of the earth'. In Acts 1:8 the little word 'and' holds the power of the Spirit together with the disciples' call to witness and mission. Let us also know in our personal experience the gift of God's Holy Spirit upon us in power! And let us therefore follow his call to engage fully in mission. Telling stories must be kept always in this double context of the power of the Spirit and witness through the proclamation of the gospel.

So let us set out on a life of storytelling for the glory of the Lord!

NOTES

1. For further stories of our time in North Sumatra, see M. Goldsmith, *Life's Tapestry* (Authentic, 1996) and E. Goldsmith, *God Can Be Trusted* (Authentic, 1997).

2. See M. Goldsmith, *Matthew and Mission: The Gospel through Jewish Eyes* (Paternoster/Jews for Jesus, 2001, 2012).

3. See M. Goldsmith, *Beyond Beards and Burqas* (IVP, 2009); Steve Bell, *Gospel for Muslims* (Authentic, 2012).

4. In a traditional Muslim cultural context, only men enjoy coffee shops.

5. In such traditional Muslim contexts, only men will gather to listen to a man teaching.

6. Every Muslim is expected to pay an annual tax on his/her property for the upkeep and charitable giving of the local mosque.

7. For an exposition of Habakkuk, see M. Goldsmith, *Any Complaints? Blame God!* (Authentic, 2008).

8. K. Kitamori, *The Theology of the Pain of God* (John Knox Press, 1965).

9. Liberation theology began in Latin America in the 1950s. At first it grew within the Roman Catholic Church, but later widened to include Christians from various denominations. It stresses liberation from oppression and poverty with a desire for justice. As a theology of the poor it was influenced by Marxism. Liberation theologians maintain that the Bible and theology must be interpreted in the light of justice and liberation from oppression.

also by Martin Goldsmith

Beyond Beards and Burqas

Connecting with Muslims
Martin Goldsmith

ISBN: 978-1-84474-410-7
160 pages, paperback

Most people live or work among Muslim colleagues and neighbours, or mingle with Islamic people on trips overseas. But many Christians struggle to see beyond the stereotypes to connect in depth with the people they meet.

In this winsome book, Martin Goldsmith recounts colourful stories from a lifetime of conversations and friendships with Muslims in various countries around the world, including the UK. Part-travelogue, part-biography, readers are whisked from an English college garden to an Afghan market, from a London secondary school to a North African tourist destination, from Dubai airport to a home in Scotland, all the while becoming better equipped to make their own connections with Muslims – to the glory of God.

Available from your local Christian bookshop or **www.thinkivp.com**

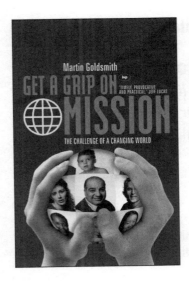

also by Martin Goldsmith

Get a Grip on Mission
The challenge of a changing world
Martin Goldsmith

ISBN: 978-1-84474-126-7
208 pages, paperback

Globalization, pluralism, urbanization and increased mobility are just some of the challenges of twenty-first-century cross-cultural mission, and Martin Goldsmith helpfully equips us to respond wisely to them. With humour, confidence and enthusiasm, he enables us to see potential barriers to mission as opportunities waiting to be grasped.

The unchanging nature of Jesus' Great Commission contrasts strongly not only with our changing world but with our dynamic God. While his commands are set in stone, his methods are not.

This book will give you fresh ideas about mission. It will help you pray, plan and advise those who want to get involved.

'Valuable alike for doers, thinkers and teachers of mission.'
Revd Dr Christopher J. H. Wright

'Martin Goldsmith brings an impassioned heart and an informed, clear mind to this most vital subject. Timely, provocative and practical.' Jeff Lucas

Available from your local Christian bookshop or **www.thinkivp.com**

Compelled by Joy

A lifelong passion for evangelism
Michael Green

ISBN: 978-1-84474-542-5
208 pages, paperback

'I was a happy teenager, content with my home, my academic success, my sporting achievements and my friendships. And I stumbled across the greatest friend of all, Jesus Christ. He is the treasure I have come to value above all else. I was not an emotional cripple looking for a crutch. I was not a romantic looking for a cause. I was not at the bottom of the pile hoping for a leg-up. I was not looking for anything in particular. But I found treasure, and that treasure has utterly transformed my life, my goals, my lifestyle ...'

Michael Green shares his passion, reflections, convictions and suggestions from a lifetime of church and university missions, not to mention numerous informal encounters.

A book to provoke, stimulate and inspire, but above all fire up every Christian for the urgent task of evangelism.

'A sparkling book – a gem and a treasure! Written by one of the most remarkable evangelists God has given to the global church in these past fifty years, it is full of wit, wisdom and experience.' Lindsay Brown

Not So Secret
Being contemporary agents for mission
Graham Orr

ISBN: 978-1-84474-591-3
160 pages, paperback

This book will help you step beyond your own familiarity with the Bible, church, doctrine, prayer and Christian jargon, and reach out to those for whom these things are completely foreign. Graham Orr's years of experience leading a church in urban Tokyo – one of the toughest places to do evangelism – have given him deep insight into how to reach those who have no knowledge of, or interest in, Christianity. Designed for those with busy urban lives, this book is full of stories, biblical insights, and ideas to put into practice.

'We are often told we need to approach the UK as a mission field. But often those voices make evangelism in a post-Christian culture seem even more difficult, and we are put off. Graham's short book changes all that. Drawing on his long and fruitful ministry in Tokyo, he shows us how, and makes us feel we can do it too.' Julian Hardyman

'Practical, spiritual and insightful ... will help us to witness more relevantly, more lovingly and with greater cultural awareness.' Martin Goldsmith, from the foreword.

Available from your local Christian bookshop or **www.thinkivp.com**

Inter-Varsity Press

For more information about IVP
and our publications visit
www.ivpbooks.com

Get regular updates at **ivpbooks.com/signup**
Find us on **facebook.com/ivpbooks**
Follow us on **twitter.com/ivpbookcentre**

Inter-Varsity Press, a company limited by guarantee registered in England and Wales, number 05202650. Registered office IVP Bookcentre, Norton Street, Nottingham NG7 3HR, United Kingdom. Registered charity number 1105757.